ROOTS IN ADOBE

Illustrated by Sam Smith

DOROTHY L. PILLSBURY

Roots

in Adobe

ALBUQUERQUE
UNIVERSITY OF NEW MEXICO PRESS

Credit is given to *The Christian Science Monitor*,
publication of the Christian Science Publishing
Society, Boston, Mass., for permission to reprint
thirty-seven articles by Dorothy Pillsbury which
originally appeared in its pages in 1952–57. "Unknown to Man" has not been published previously.
Appreciation is extended to the New Mexico State
Board of Education, Santa Fe, for permission to
include "Magic Carpets" and "Mysteries of 'Learning Paper'" which first appeared in *Education
Without Reservations,* a report of the New Mexico
Developmental Education Program, 1956, prepared
by Clarence M. Hill and Dorothy Pillsbury.

TABLE OF CONTENTS

BUT EVER THE ESSENCE

*O*netime residents of Santa Fe and the surrounding region gasp with dismay when they return and see the changes that have taken place through the years. "Three sides of the Plaza are ruined," they cry. "Look at those blatant neon lights on some of the stores at night. Don't tell me you have traffic lights and parking meters. And TV antennas on top of adobe houses! Even in the Spanish *placitas!* What has become of all the burros with wood on their backs? Does every Indian drive a pickup truck now? There goes an elderly señora with a permanent and no shawl over it."

However, returning residents do not complain about the hard-surfaced highways over which most of them re-entered the region. A quarter of a century ago, most of these roads were precarious enough to deter all but the stout-

1

hearted. Even the few miles from Santa Fe to the Spanish villages of Truchas and Trampas back in the mountains were something of an adventure. People bragged about having been there. It was a little like penetrating Tibet.

When I first moved into the Little Adobe House, nearly every *casita* in Tenorio Flat was faintly illumined at night by kerosene lamps and there wasn't a street light anywhere around. Flashlights or lanterns made of an old tin can shielding a candle were standard equipment for evening visiting. Burros braying were my morning alarm clock. Antonito led his goats across my front yard to nibble dried shrubs and grasses on a winter day. My door key grew rusty for lack of use and windows could be left wide open for day or night absences. The ugly word "prowler" was not in our vocabulary.

Since the war, our old town has been growing, house by house and subdivision by subdivision—modern houses. Adobe houses involving mostly hand work have become practically antiques as they cost twice as much to build as their cement-block substitutes. Returning residents sigh and exclaim, "Yes, the old town has changed." Then they hasten to add almost against their will, "But it still has its charm." To which some residents answer confidently, "Our old town and the region around it have deep roots."

A game something like musical chairs has been going on here for some years. Young Spanish Americans, prosperous in business, professions or politics, buy modern homes equipped with every modern gadget. At the same time, Anglos, embittered with changes in their land of dreams, are avidly buying the ancestral adobes of the Spanish people. Some of these ancient adobes under acquisitive Anglo hands are turning into semblances of household museums unlike anything a real *paisano* ever inhabited.

Santa Fe, slowly approaching forty thousand population, scattered about with much vacant land within its limits and awe-inspiring space without, contains some of the most vociferous people on the planet. Just let any group of progressives try to change something and the pack is in full cry. Petitions carry impressive signatures, the City Council finds its meetings invaded by oratory and membership in the Old Santa Fe Association zooms.

The din of battle became quite terrific a few years ago when it was suggested that *Acequia Madre,* a narrow, winding road not far from the Little Adobe House, should have its spring-breaking chuckholes smoothed a bit. On one side of the road runs the old Spanish ditch that once carried water from the nearby mountains to the Spanish-Colonial settlement of Santa Fe. Alas, for many dry years, that ditch had carried little water and had become the repository for much litter. Why not make a complete job of it? Why not cut down the bordering trees and thickets of wild roses? Why not fill in the old ditch and widen the road while removing the chuckholes?

Santa Fe went quite wild. Wealthy citizens wintering in warmer climes spent recklessly for telegrams and long-distance calls to everyone in authority. Letters appeared in the local paper that were written practically in iambic pentameters. The old road still has its Spanish ditch—and its chuckholes. Great is the rejoicing, even though we all know it is but temporary, since *Acequia Madre* is again listed for paving.

With all the uproar, no matter who wins or loses, a certain something remains. Spanish still floats along our crooked, narrow streets. Indians still spread their handiwork under the *portál* of the old Palace of the Governors which has, itself, weathered an Indian revolt and four different flags. Adobe houses which show no evidence of being household museums, still shelter many of

4

us—Indians, Spanish and Anglos, each in his own version. The tempo of our living goes on at a more leisurely pace than is customary elsewhere and the sly fetters of standardization have not yet bound us.

Even returning, onetime residents soon hush their bewailing and exclaim, "There is something here after all. Santa Fe is still Santa Fe," and then they ask, "What is it?"

Part of that "something" is, without a doubt, the natural grandeur and beauty of the old town's setting. Part of it is the brush strokes of a glamorous history. Part of it is due to archaeologists who have laboriously uncovered the footsteps of "those who are gone" and thereby given us a perspective of some depth.

Indian descendants of "those who are gone" are still here in increasing numbers in spite of great vicissitudes. Descendants of Spanish colonists are still here in spite of arid soil and a once-terrible isolation. The region continues to draw and hold its own—including modern Americans.

But the greatest part of that "something" is, amusingly enough, the very factor which many of us most deplore. The essence is change—change caused by impact of races and peoples and cultures on one another through the centuries.

*H*ow happy-go-lucky these Spanish people are," many Anglos exclaim, somewhat wistfully. "In times like these, it must be wonderful to have them around."

To illustrate this alleged happy-go-lucky quality, an Anglo told the story of the Pacheco family and their fiesta under the morning stars. "That Pacheco family had a little ranch near our country home back in the hills. A few years ago, in a summer of great drought, they received their share of ditch water. It was evidently so meager that they just let it run where it would and called in their friends to make a fiesta under the cotton-wood trees sometime between midnight and sunrise. They had a fire and we could hear them laughing and singing under the morning stars. It sounded out of this world.

"When my husband got his share of ditch water, it was so little, he fussed and fumed for days. It was not enough for even our grounds. So how could it have been enough for the Pacheco ranch? But did they fuss and fume about it? No, they made a fiesta and sang happily until daylight."

The true story of the Pacheco fiesta is quite different. Like many Spanish-American country people, they are subsistence farmers. Their *ranchito* is a long, narrow piece of land with an *acequia,* water ditch, along the upper narrow end. That means that the furrows for the water are quite long and in time of meager flow, the precious *agua* does not reach the lower end of the land at all.

Jacobo Pacheco had managed to keep things alive until mid-August. Everything depended on the August run of water. Closest to the *acequia* came the fruit trees. Would there be enough water for his peach, pear and apple trees? If the fruit reached any size, he could sell it for a good price along the highway under a *ramada* he had built there. That would mean new overalls and shoes for all the *muchachos.* Would there, oh, would there be a little water for his bean and chile plants just below the orchard? If there was, it would mean they would eat next winter. Further down were planted the rows of corn and last of all, *las calabasas,* squashes. Oh, if there would be a few droplets even for *las calabasas!*

For days, Jacobo and his twin boys, twelve-years-old Juanito *y* Tomascito, worked under the summer sun to get their parched land ready for whatever water might come down the ditch. Jacobo with his rickety, horse-drawn plough made deep, straight furrows. With battered shovels and hoes, he and the boys made encircling basins for the bean and chile plants, for the corn and *las calabasas.* All were connected by an intricate system of little furrows. They made a high embankment at the end of the *ranchito.* They filled up gopher holes with rocks and adobe mud. They made ready every inch of their land for water, even if the prospects for receiving it were not bright.

Water came languidly into their *acequia* at six o'clock one blistering morning. But there was very little water. It trickled into the furrows between the fruit trees. The ground was powder-dry and soaked up so much water on either side of the furrows that little was left to run down to the lower trees, let alone the bean and chile plants.

All that August day, Jacobo and his little boys walked the furrows, coaxing, guiding water along. Not a drop was lost. At nightfall, Jacobo sent the boys to the house. Angelita, their mother, fed them and they dropped in their muddy overalls on their bed. When all her children were asleep, Angelita pinned up her skirts and walked the furrows with Jacobo. The orchard, at last, had soaked up enough water. The leaves on the trees were uncurling. Jacobo opened the furrows into the bean and chile patches. At ten o'clock, Angelita could work no longer. From then on until midnight, Jacobo walked the furrows alone, using all the skill and patience that had come down to him through hundreds of years of farming in an arid land.

Shortly after that strange hush that comes to country places after midnight, he burst into the house. Angelita, her bare, brown feet covered with mud, was asleep in a chair. "Angelita," cried Jacobo, "the water has reached the corn rows. A little trickle has reached *las calabasas!* It has reached *las calabasas!*"

"*Gracias a Diós,*" breathed Angelita, leaping to her feet and shaking the sleepy twins. "Juanito, Tomascito, wake up. The water has reached *las calabasas!* We make fiesta! Each of you jump on a horse. One of you ride to the adobe of Señor Manzanares up the road. The other ride to the adobe of Señor Montoya down the road. Tell them to come *pronto*. We make fiesta. Tell them the water has reached *las calabasas!*"

She built a fire in the old wood-burning stove. She set a huge kettle of beans and chile to rewarming. She fried *tortillas*. She opened her few remaining jars of last year's peaches. She made hot chocolate, shaking in cinnamon. She slipped pans of *bizcochitos* sprinkled with *anís* into the oven.

Jacobo built a little fire under the cottonwood trees knowing that the dawn breezes would have a chill. The younger children were picked up, bedding and all, and deposited around the fire where they blinked their big eyes and laughed at the winging flames.

At two o'clock in the morning, the farm wagons of the Manzanares and Montoya families rolled in. They were packed with big-hatted men and shawl-wrapped women and numerous hilarious children. "Did the water reach *las calabasas?*" demanded the men as they jumped from high wagon seats. Jacobo took them to see for themselves. It was only a little trickle around the woolly-leaved plants, but it had four hours to trickle. It could not get away.

In the circle of firelight they ate *con mucho gusto*. They laughed; they chattered about nothing at all. They sang *Allá en el Rancho Grande* over and over again with support from two mouth organs and a *guitarra* with a missing string. Happy they were as if a suddenly called fiesta under the morning stars were the most natural of social events.

But these people are not go-lucky. Their ancestors would not have kept the tiny flame of European culture alight in an arid land in a red man's world had they been go-lucky. Essence of this land of mountain heights and desert waste, of straight-topped mesas and purple buttes, of rusty pink arroyos and illimitable space, how happy, how gallantly have you gone!

IMPACT & IMMUTABLE ROOTS

*W*hen Luz, one of Mrs. Apodaca's older daughters, and her *caballero* moved into their own home in another part of town, I thought I detected a gleam in her mother's eyes. "You take that beeg stove you bought for me when you were working," she offered magnanimously. "Your keetchen ees beeger than mine and you will need that beeg stove to cook nize things for all the friends and relatives who come to see you."

Luz and her husband, Remedio, bought ready-built a small adobe from someone who was moving away. Unlike most adobe houses, it had a small entrance hall at the front door. In that hall there stand side-by-side but three furnishings. One is a huge electric refrigerator. The second is a hot-water heater operated by electricity and the third is a resplendent electric washing machine.

In addition to city water and electricity, the house could easily have connection with a nearby gas line. But at that, Luz reverts to type. In her big sunny kitchen with its red print curtains, geraniums blooming in tin cans and strands of chiles hanging from pine-tree ceiling beams, stands that enormous cookstove that burns wood. "Things taste better cooked with wood," declares Luz, "and besides, that big wood stove warms the whole house in cold weather. And no gas bills to pay!"

I knew that Luz paid for those evidences of modernity, one by one, by dint of work in Anglo homes. As a girl she had worked briefly in a dress shop, but as a married woman she reverted to type and trotted through my yard, housework-bent. When the appliances were paid for, she worked no more.

When her three little boys had reached school age, she plunged into great activity again in Anglo households. The following summer she bought new clothing for herself and the boys and started by bus for a vacation in California. They ate in the biggest and most crowded of cafeterias, saw pictures in the most ornate of movie palaces, took sight-seeing trips to Hollywood and waded fearfully about on the fringe of the vast Pacific.

13

"It was nice," declared Luz mildly, "but *demasiado*—too, too much. And in not one of those fine cafeterias do they know how to cook red beans right. Nothing like red beans and chile simmered and simmered on a good wood stove. I could hardly wait to get home to cook some. But, Señora, isn't it terrible the trouble we have nowadays to get real piñón wood? Yellow pine, *sabina*—cedar that goes pop like firecrackers, anything but piñón that burns so long and smells so good."

One night the following autumn, Luz burst into my house in a state of great excitement and with her clothes in a most bedraggled condition. She was wearing an old dress and an apron that were ripped and torn and covered with dirt. The new permanent was standing on end in some places and hanging limply in others. Her face, hands and bare brown legs were scratched and cut. "You should see what we have on a big red truck out in front of Mamacita's house," she exclaimed, waving her arms and laughing. "Piñón wood, all that the truck will hold!"

"Where did you find so much piñón wood?" I demanded.

"From Mrs. Kit, an Anglo lady I used to work for before she moved out of town. She wanted to keep a horse to ride and lots of dogs. So she moved out in the hills where the little piñón trees grow. Some of those piñón trees on her place had been burned by lightning, some crowded the little trees, some hid the view from her windows. So she told my husband we could have them for wood if we would cut them down and take them away. I was so excited about getting some real piñón wood that I went along to help. I worked all day, and look at me."

Luz sank happily into the big rocker. "Mind if I wait here until Remedio finds a man on the Camino who has a power saw? He is going to walk up there and let the truck stand."

I put some chocolate on to heat and investigated the contents of my cookie jar. "But where did you get the big truck?" I asked, shaking cinnamon into the hot chocolate.

"Oh," exulted Luz, "that belongs to another friend. We give him one-half of the piñón wood from those trees, to take his truck and crosscut saw and help us. The men cut down the trees and I helped trim them with my little saw and clippers. Nothing in that truck but good thick trunks of piñón!"

Between sips of hot chocolate and bites of cookie, Luz chattered like a school girl. "Never did I have such a good time, Señora. The sky so blue, the air so sweet, the sun so warm! Work, work, laugh, laugh, sing, sing—all of us! I tell my husband that the next time we have a good crop of piñón nuts, we will take our boys out to the forests to gather those nuts just as we used to do. They are missing too much. I want them to remember the piñón forests. Wherever they go when they grow up, they can keep a little of New Mexico if they remember the smell of sun on piñón trees."

"I hope Remedio will find the man with the power saw," I worried. "It will take more than a handsaw and axe to work up those hard piñón trunks."

"He'll find," laughed Luz. "He will give him half of our share of the wood to saw it all up."

"But that will leave you only a quarter of the piñón wood for all your hard work," I protested.

"Sure," agreed Luz in amazement. "And out of our quarter we will give Mamacita a big box full. And another big box for you, Señora. Oh, yes we will. We know how you like piñón wood for your fireplace. We *want* you to have it. And a few other boxes for Cousin Canuto and the Seguras and some other people."

16

Came a loud honking from the direction where the big red truck was waiting. Luz hurried toward the door. "A million thanks, Señora. Never was chocolate so good." Then she glanced at her adobe-and-pitch-stained dress and apron. "I'll just pop these duds into the washing machine," she said easily.

LAST OF LOS LEÑADORES

*B*urros were once as common in Santa Fe as blue-winged piñón jays. They brayed from all points of the compass with rasping plaintiveness just before dawn. They plodded up and down the narrow, crooked streets of the old town, so laden with piñón wood that only their fuzzy ears and delicate little feet could be seen. In their leisure hours they invaded gardens, even those of the gubernatorial mansion, and consumed most of the dahlias.

In charge of each string of burros was a *leñador*, woodchopper, a man in ragged, pitch-stained clothing, worn shoes and tattered hat. He drove his burros out to the pigmy forests, cut down the trees, chopped the wood in fireplace lengths, loaded it on the backs of his protesting burros and plodded slowly back into Santa Fe. Here he led the string of big-eared animals from house to house. There followed bargaining, laughter, and the exchange of news and sometimes the clink of money.

But as automobiles and people increased along the narrow streets of Santa Fe, there was little room left for heavily-laden strings of burros. Added to that was the fact that more and more Anglos had joined the fireplace cult and needed wood, not by the burroload, but by the truckload. Then one by one, *leñadores* and burros disappeared. The dahlias in the governor's gardens bloomed untouched.

On the wall of the Little Adobe House is a picture of burros laden with wood. When Cousin Canuto noticed it for the first time, it brought back exciting memories. "Did you know, Señora, that my father was the last of *los leñadores?* When I was a boy I used to go with him out in the piñón forests to get the good wood. We camped there for many days and then brought it into Santa Fe with our string of burros. We had our regular customers and every sale was a visit, too. We lived way out in the country then and saw few people. Ah, being *un leñador* was a highly respected profession!

"When the big woodyards and trucks took over the wood business, *los leñadores* disappeared one by one. The woodyard people offered to send

19

their big trucks out to the forests to buy the wood we had cut. But our profession was greater than that. The best part of it was going from adobe to adobe, hearing news, laughing and joking. We just gave up and disappeared and so did our burros."

A few days later, I saw María Lupita, Cousin Canuto's wife, and Mrs. Apodaca passing by with shawl-wrapped heads close together. This usually is an indication that Cousin Canuto is off on another outrageous project. But this time their shawls were not closely wrapped about them like protecting armor. They were blowing out behind them like wings. The two women were laughing, chattering and gesticulating with dramatic, small brown hands. Cousin Canuto was up to something again, something of which his womenfolk evidently approved. Another thing puzzled me. On several mornings before dawn, I thought I heard, at some distance, the rasping bray of vocalizing burros.

At last Mrs. Apodaca, fairly scintillating with excitement, burst into my house. "Ah, Señora, do you know what ees now my Cousin Canuto? Ah, Señora, you should see heem. Not hees papá, but my Cousin Canuto ees now last of *los leñadores*. Four burritos he found back in a mountain village. You should see heem—old *pantalones*, fleece-lined coat, beeg old hat weeth torn brim, piñón wood on backs of burritos!"

"Tell him," I interrupted, "I want to be his first customer. I will take all four burroloads of piñón wood."

Mrs. Apodaca shook her head violently. "It ees not for sale. It ees for *la atmósfera.*"

At that point, in burst the last of *los leña-dores* in full costume but mercifully without burritos.

"That little picture of yours, Señora," exclaimed Cousin Canuto, "gave me the start. I owe you much, Señora, and I will repay you magnificently. Soon I will have much money."

"But how," I asked, "can you make any money if you won't sell your piñón wood?"

"Señora, you should see those burritos. I brush their coats. I oil their hoofs. María Lupita make little tassels of blue, red and orange yarn to dangle from bridles. Behold me, Señora, when the season of *turistas* is here, leading my four beautiful burritos where wander *las turistas* seeking shots for their cameras. Gladly will they pay me a dollar for a few shots. In a single day, I can easily make twenty or thirty dollars. When the Bureau of *Turistas* hears what I am doing to bring back *la atmósfera* of old Santa Fe, they will, without doubt, put me on a steady salary as well."

Then for days and weeks nothing at all happened. Mrs. Apodaca was plainly avoiding me. No sounds of rasping burro braying came to me at dawn. At last, Cousin Canuto in usual attire paused in a hurried passage through my yard. "What has become of *la atmósfera?*" I questioned.

22

"Oh," said Cousin Canuto easily, "Burros are livestock and there is a law against keeping them in the city limits now. And besides," added Cousin Canuto proudly, "the City Council felt that such crowds would gather about me and my burritos that the traffic of Santa Fe would be completely blocked. As it probably would be. I had to drive those burritos back to their village."

"*Ay de mí,*" I groaned.

"When I was driving them home," beamed Cousin Canuto, "a man saw us and took many pictures. He is sending them to some contest of picture-taking. He will, of course, win first prize. He gave me five dollars in advance. I go now to town to buy soda pop and ice cream. We give a party tonight in *mi tienda,* my store. Do come, Señora, and help us celebrate."

"Celebrate what?" I demanded.

In ragged blue jeans, worn shirt and shoes, Cousin Canuto drew himself up to an elegant pose. "That winning photograph will hang in some great art gallery. It will be printed in many fine magazines. Tonight, Señora, we celebrate FAME."

23

*P*assing through my yard, Cousin Canuto often stops to admire the hand-carved gate which leads to the walled patio of the violinist. Cousin Canuto acknowledges agreeably that the gate and its carving have their good points. Then he usually adds, "Ah, Señora, I wish you might have seen the gateway *magnífica* of my Tío Perfecto."

According to Cousin Canuto, Uncle Perfecto labored for a dozen winters to build and to carve with intricate designs the gate that stood at the entrance to his *ranchito*.

When I inquire where that *ranchito* might be found, Cousin Canuto shakes his head sadly. "Alas, Señora, my Tío Perfecto and his wife María Escolástica, have long since departed from this earth and their many children have scattered I know not where. I knew them when I was a little boy. Their *ranchito*, I am told, has been abandoned and the pine forest, in which it stood far back in the mountains, has taken over all evidences of habitation. The road to it was not built for the low *carros* of today but for wood wagons drawn by horses. Maybe a jeep could make it or an old high-slung *Fordcito*. Even the nearest village whose name was Tranquilidád has been completely deserted. I often wonder what became of that monstrous gate of Tío Perfecto."

The two swinging portions of the gate, according to Cousin Canuto, were higher than a tall man's head and thicker than the length of his index finger. They were held together when closed by a great hand-wrought iron hasp. At nightfall, Tío Perfecto walked the quarter-mile from his tiny adobe house to his imposing gateway and secured the two halves with a ponderous padlock. Each morning he walked that quarter-mile again to insert an enormous key in the huge padlock and fling open the gate. It was a kind of daily ritual which must have given the little subsistence farmer some sense of living in a castle in Spain.

Little by little, I learned from Cousin Canuto that the imposing hand-carved gate had occasioned some unhappiness in the family of Tío Perfecto. All the many winters he had sat by the warm kitchen stove, smoothing the huge timbers and carving them with intricate designs of leaves and flowers, Tía María Escolástica frowned and complained that she had to do most of the work on the *ranchito*. Aunt María had to go out through the deep snows to milk the goats, feed the chickens, bring in wood and toss hay to the two rough-coated horses.

When the sons and daughters of Tío Perfecto acquired enough years, one by one they left the *ranchito* to find work in the big towns of the state and to establish their own homes—probably without hand-carved gates.

In spite of myself, my sympathy was not with the lonely and hard-working María Escolástica nor with the children who knew no other playmates than one another. That little subsistence farmer who spent most of the year plowing, planting and garnering his forest-bound acres, preempted the winter months to give some tangible form to the dreams of his heart and some sense of grandeur to his monotonous life.

I searched maps to see if I could find the location of the village of Tranquilidád; I questioned road department men and forest rangers. No one knew of any enormous hand-carved gates lost in a forgotten mountain pocket.

One late winter afternoon when "Mees" Emily and I were sitting by the red-faced corner fireplace, I told her the story I had gathered bit by bit from Cousin Canuto's youthful memories. So intent was I on relating the story that had become unreasonably poignant to me that I did not glance in her direction until I had finished. Then I realized that her face was flushed with excitement. "I know that *ranchito*," she gasped. "I've seen that great hand-carved gate. It must have been when we first came to New Mexico, twenty-five or more years ago. My daughter and I did a lot of prowling around in an old high-slung Ford. We carried food and blankets and extra gasoline and oil as we were always losing ourselves.

"I'll never forget the day we came up through the pine forest and saw that beautifully carved gate, badly weathered, but still intact. The enormous padlock was rusted, but tightly closed. The adobe house, barn, and chicken shelters had melted away with winter snows and summer rains. There was not much left of them but their crumbling foundations. Little pine trees were growing on what had once been cleared fields and mountain pastures. I remember that the place was full of bird song and fragrant with the scent of wild roses."

I sat drinking in "Mees" Emily's words. I
felt strangely elated. At last I asked, "I suppose
the adobe wall that held that hand-carved gate
had crumbled away like the little house? How did
the gate manage to stand up?"

"Mees" Emily looked at me knowingly.
"The gate was held up by two enormous posts

sunk deeply in the ground. They sagged a little, but still upheld the gate."

Came a long silence. Then "Mees" Emily said gently, "There never had been a wall around the *ranchito*. We looked carefully for signs of crumbled adobe such as outlined the foundations of the adobe house and barn. There was no such evidence—none whatever. We drove right around that well-padlocked gate. I think Tío Perfecto or anyone else could have done the same thing. He evidently put all the time he had into carving that beautiful gate and never got around to building a wall."

The next time Cousin Canuto passed through my yard, I dashed out and stopped him. "Your Tío Perfecto must have had a wall around his *ranchito* with the enormous hand-carved gate?"

"No, Señora," answered Cousin Canuto unconcerned. "There was no wall at all. Just two great beams to hold up the gate! Carving the gate was the activity *importante*."

TIMBER LINE

*E*ver since I have been going into Cousin Canuto's combination home and little store, I have vaguely noticed a piece of hand-wrought timber propped on end in an adobe corner. Today I was visiting him because I had heard from Mrs. Apodaca that the picture of *los* burritos and the last of the woodchoppers had evidently taken no prize. Not even an honorable mention. Fame was still a delusion and a cheat.

But Cousin Canuto seemed absolutely unconcerned. Seeing my eyes on the great timber, Cousin Canuto remarked, "That heavy pole was the tongue on my grandfather's wood-wagon. Ah, that wood-wagon. It hauled heavy loads for all the village—rocks, sacks of grain, and adobe bricks. Sit down, Señora, and I'll tell you the story."

A shawl-wrapped neighbor, after prolonged inspection, selected three yellow onions, two potatoes, and a box of marshmallow-topped cookies, and placed them on the store's rough little counter.

Cousin Canuto paid not the slightest attention to his customer, but brought up two rickety chairs to the little black stove and settled down for a pleasant interlude.

The customer waited patiently in black-wrapped silence. At last she coughed timidly to attract attention. Cousin Canuto kept right on polishing two red apples to add zest to our story-telling hour. The customer coughed again which brought María Lupita on the run from her kitchen, a dripping spoon in one hand and a dish towel in the other. She wrote on a slip of paper the customer's name, the items she had bought, and the price. Then she impaled the paper on a great nail in the wall behind the counter which was Cousin Canuto's simple method of credit bookkeeping.

At last Cousin Canuto asked, "Have you ever been in the village of Trampas in the shadow of Truchas Peaks, Señora?"

"Countless times!" I remembered the lovely old village on the edge of a deep valley, looking as if it were ready to take off in limitless turquoise space to sail to the thirteen-thousand foot summits of the Truchas Peaks.

"My grandfather's family settled there among the earlier Spanish colonists. It was rough going even in his day, shut off by almost impassable roads from the rest of the world. When my grandfather had many years, the tongue of his wood-wagon broke. It was not worth mending. Some of the younger men offered to go back in the forests and cut down a suitable tree to make a new wagon tongue. But my grandfather said only he could find the kind of timber that was needed.

"My Aunt Louisita, in whose home he lived, gave Grandfather a warm hand-woven blanket, as winter was almost upon us. She filled a big jar with red beans, meat and chile and a box with freshly fried *tortillas* for his lonely campfire in the deep forest. The old man sharpened his ax and started out one wind-shrieking morning. I had never seen him look so happy.

"No one expected him home the first night. But when the second and third nights had passed and he had not returned, search parties went out from our village and that of neighboring Truchas. After fruitless hours, the men returned shaking their heads and talking of deep rock-lined arroyos, of slippery steep trails, and of stalking mountain lions. It was a very bad time for our village. Women visited from house to house, whispering behind their black shawls. Only my Aunt Louisita kept smilingly about her work—cooking more beans, meat, and chile and frying more *tortillas* against Grandfather's return.

"Just about sunset on the fourth day, Grandfather appeared with a great gnarled piece of tree trunk over his shoulder. Immediately the men in the village began to berate Grandfather for causing them to be anxious about him and to take so much time from gathering the last of their crops.

"But Grandfather placed that piece of heavy tree trunk by the corner fireplace, ate an enormous supper of my aunt's good cooking, and went to bed without answering any questions. His eyes twinkled like the coals in the fireplace and the corners of his eyebrows turned up like little arrows.

"Not until after breakfast next morning would he answer any of the young men's questions. Then he picked up that gnarled piece of timber. 'Feel the weight of that in your hands, *mis amigos*,' he urged. 'Does that feel like wood grown in a pretty pine-sheltered valley? A valley where flowers grow and the deer leads her fawn to drink from a gentle stream! Where does a man go to find a piece of timber like this? Up high, high on the mountain side where few trees grow, where the eagle spreads its wings and the great storms blow. That's the place to find a piece of wood like this."

Cousin Canuto ate his last bite of apple. "My grandfather worked all that storm-lashed winter —smoothing, shaping, almost grain by grain, forming a wagon tongue from that strong timber. It served the village well for many years, even until the truckies came in. Then the home there was broken up. But I went back and found that old wagon pole and brought it to my home."

Cousin Canuto and I sat silently. Then he said, "Timber line, where great storms shout and exult, produces its own kind of trees. They are of a great persistency and of a toughness."

THAT CARMENCITA SOARS AGAIN

*S*eñora," asked Mrs. Apodaca, "What ees Gracie-us Leeving?"

I could not recognize the words with the Spanish accent and intonation my neighbor gave them. "Come and see," she begged. "That Carmencita has something in her room she calls Gracie-us Leeving and I do not want eet to spread all over my *casita.*"

Dramatically she flung open the door to the thick-walled little room her youngest and most perplexing daughter had inherited from her older sisters, Lupe, Luz and Armendita, now all married and in their own homes. With accusing finger she pointed to a low couch in a corner. "Hollywood couch," she explained, "in place of good iron bed with lamb's-wool mattress and blanket I weave on my own loom. That bed I paint any color my girls like—pink for Lupe, purple for Luz and green for Armendita. But that Carmencita buys hard, cheap box couch and saws off legs so ees almost on floor. She makes cover for it weeth petticoat all around. 'Eef you have to sleep so close to floor to make Gracie-us Leeving,' I tale her, 'why not sleep on pile of blankets on floor the way *los indios* used to do?' "

A brown shaking finger pointed to a place where a battered chest of drawers once stood. It too, I remembered, had also seen many coats of paint: pink for Lupe, purple for Luz and green for Armendita. But it had disappeared. "Dressing table," explained Mrs. Apodaca. "Made out of wooden boxes and petticoats all around like Hollywood couch. For a *muchacha* who goes around in ragged old blue jeans and no-shape sweater and flat-heeled no-shine shoes, of what use ees a dressing table? When Lupe, Luz and Armendita were same years as Carmencita, they put up hair on curlers and work to make *dinero* to buy pretty dress.

"And now," groaned Mrs. Apodaca, wringing small brown hands, "that Carmencita geeves her papá no peace. He must take crowbar and knock out whole side of wall and put in glass so Carmencita can have what she call picture window." Mrs. Apodaca peered anxiously through the small panes of the deep-set window. "I can see no picture, Señora. Only my clotheslines weeth papá's underwear on eet and a corner of the Segura goat corral."

On the big kitchen table which Carmencita had significantly retained and which serves as desk and work table, I noticed a great stack of magazines given to household beautification. They had evidently been contributed by an Anglo lady where Carmencita had acted as baby-sitter.

A great light illuminated the situation. "It's Gracious Living," I pronounced carefully. "Those magazines started the whole flight toward Hollywood couch, dressing table and picture window."

"What does Gracious Living mean?" begged Mrs. Apodaca, still bewildered.

"It means living with beauty and—and grace," I explained feebly. Then I added, "Those two words are the cause for more extravagances and harassed husbands than any other two words in the English language."

Mrs. Apodaca stood twisting the big silver ring on her index finger. "Eef reading the Anglo *periódicos* started Carmencita on all thees," she sighed, "I wish some Anglo lady would geeve her a beeg, beeg stack of *periódicos* that would make her curl her hair and care how she look. Do they have *periódicos* like that, Señora?"

"Hundreds of them," I encouraged. "You know how Carmencita soars when the breeze of a new idea lifts her wings. The next stack of old magazines she brings home, let me know. I can probably chart a pretty accurate curve of what we may next expect."

Nothing happened for weeks. Carmencita played her flute, collected news items for "curren' events" class, sold small commodities from door to door, entered several advertising contests, babysat, and clad in ragged blue jeans and much-washed sweater, pedaled her bicycle all over town on missions of evident moment.

At last Mrs. Apodaca reported that Carmencita had acquired a "beeg, beeg" stack of Anglo *periódicos* and was reading them far into the night. The only change that Mrs. Apodaca could report was that Carmencita seemed to be "theenking, theenking." When Carmencita "theenks" and "theenks," Santa Fe's Tenorio Flat is usually treated to what approximates an atomic explosion.

Breathlessly I dashed over to *Casita* Apodaca to examine the "beeg, beeg" stack of Anglo *periódicos*. One hasty glance was enough. The entire stack consisted of space fiction.

Seeing my look of consternation, Mrs. Apodaca inquired hopefully, "Do the Anglo *periódicos* tell a girl how to make the curls and have the pretty dresses?"

"Not exactly," I groaned.

"What are they about, Señora?"

"They deal with interstellar space, Mrs. Apodaca—the limitless space between the stars, the greater and the lesser planets, the flight there in space ships, and a description of beings and scenery found on those planets."

Mrs. Apodaca bound her shawl more tightly about her head as if she already felt the winds that blow between the stars. I sat entranced reading bits of superb description of what no one had ever seen. Came the clatter of a bicycle cast negligently to the ground and Carmencita flung herself into the room.

"Mamacita," she shouted, "guess where I've been. Down to the place where you go if you want to join the U Esse Air Force. Did you know, Señora, that girls can join the U Esse Air Force? A nice man talked to me. He said I would have to finish school and know a lot of arithmetic and spelling and geography and U Esse history. He said he was glad I was so good in curren' events. Papá will be glad. I can't bother with a picture window now."

In the course of a few weeks, Carmentita's appearance and manner have changed. She has wrapped her long braids snugly about her head. She has bought trim little skirts and jackets. Her new shoes twinkle with daily polishing. When she meets me along Chamisa Road, she gives me a snappy salute and strides purposefully along her way. Even now she is soaring in the spaces between the stars.

SILVER SLIPPERS

*A*fter the family of young Mr. Abeyta returned to a ranch near Santa Fe, he and Carmencita resumed their friendship as if three years had not intervened. They rode their bicycles at top speed through my yard as if bent for activities of great importance. Little by little Carmencita's near-military shoes lost their high polish and were eventually replaced by the discarded canvas "sneakers." Soon she was wearing the faded, patched blue jeans and shapeless sweaters of pre-military days. Her braids flew out behind her as she whizzed by on her dilapidated bicycle. Carmencita had reverted to the tomboy.

Mrs. Apodaca was not so unhappy over this reversion as I had expected her to be. Anything that would take Carmencita's attention from Space was worth the price according to her mother.

Young Mr. Abeyta's appearance had changed during his three years' absence. No longer did he affect the South American *vaquero* costume used when he rode his old white horse clumping along the dirt roads of Santa Fe. Now he wore young ranchman's attire—blue jeans tucked into high boots, loud-checked woolen shirts with louder neckerchief, and a ten-gallon hat slightly turned up on the sides. If possible, he was more handsome in this costume than as a *vaquero*. He was quite grown up.

"Those Abeyta boys," sighed Mrs. Apodaca, "I remember them as babies. Five of them like little stair steps! And each new one more *guapo*—handsome—than the last. Young Mr. Abeyta is the youngest of them all."

"Where do Carmencita and Young Mr. Abeyta go when they pedal so fast through my yard?" I asked.

Mrs. Apodaca smiled. "He show Carmencita *ranchitos* where they have ploughing of the contour, the crops that rotate, leetle deetches that have the cément not to waste water like old dirt deetch and how to grow alfalfa. He goes to school of the farming."

Mrs. Apodaca sat rocking and "theenking." "Ees better, Señora," she burst out, "that young people keep feet on good red *tierra* and do not theenk too much about Space. Space pay no grocery beels and beelds no nize adobe house. How a *muchacho muy guapo* like Young Mr. Abeyta can be seen weeth girl dressed like my Carmencita, I know not. But even old blue jeans and washed-out sweater ees better than military skirt, jacket, shoes and mind feexed on Space. Maybe he theenk she look all right on *ranchito*."

Then one day, Carmencita tapped at my door. "Please, Señora, can I use telephone? I go to formal dance at High-School Homecoming and I want to make appointment for permanent."

I looked with dismay at Carmencita's long blue-black braids. "You're not going to cut off those braids?" I protested.

"Only a little. I'm going to have a long page-boy bob with the ends curled under."

In a few nights, she came dancing over with silver slippers on her feet and a pale-pink dress covered with net ruffles that rippled like moon-light from short puffed sleeves to hem of full skirt. Her hair, too, rippled in waves across her shoulders.

"It's all nice but this old white coat I have to wear," she complained. "I had to borrow it from Luz. It looks terrible. Too big and too old-

43

looking!" Then she giggled. "Mamacita offered me her best black shawl. But I thought that would be even worse."

"Shawl, shawl," I exclaimed. "Of course you should wear a shawl. Wait a minute. I have my grandmother's wedding shawl. It is a real China shawl—ivory white with long heavy fringe and gorgeous embroidery."

Carmencita gasped with joy when she saw it. "Mind if I fold it this way?" A little breeze fluttered as she flung the ancient shawl about her shoulders. One fold was pulled over her head, a corner was wrapped with inherited, graceful gesture about her throat. That shawl might have started out as a China shawl like those which Yankee sea captains brought from the Orient on full-sailed ships to their womenfolk. But on Carmencita, it had become as Spanish as a black lace *mantilla*. She floated out of the door like a white cloud edged with pink, skimming on silver slippers that seemed never to touch the ground.

In a day or two, Mrs. Apodaca brought my grandmother's shawl back to the Little Adobe House. I had expected to see her in a blissful state of happiness following Carmencita's beautiful appearance for the dance with a *caballero muy guapo* of whom I knew she approved.

44

"*Si,*" she answered my inquiries, "that Carmencita have fine time at dance. *Si,* she look nize. *Muchas gracias* for the so-beautiful shawl." And then she was silent.

"And Young Mr. Abeyta," I questioned, "must have looked very, very handsome with her?"

"Oh, Mr. Abeyta looked *guapo,*" she admitted. "All the Abeyta boys are *guapo.* Only it wasn't Young Mr. Abeyta who went to the dance. It was an older brother."

"I suppose he, too, talked about alfalfa in the field and cément in the water ditches!"

"He deed not," contradicted Mrs. Apodaca sadly.

"What did he talk about? What is he going to be when he's through school?"

"Be pilot on Space plane," whispered Mrs. Apodaca.

Then she wound herself up in her shawl like a mummy and plodded heavily homeward. She wore no silver slippers.

PROCESSION THROUGH THE SNOW

$\mathcal{T}$he footpath which starts opposite my driveway leads by many twists and turns to Cousin Canuto's *placita*. Up and down that snowy footpath goes Cousin Canuto, muffled in his worn sheepskin coat and topped by his big felt hat, whose brim sags with the weight of accumulated precipitation. Cousin Canuto is apparently unconcerned with weather conditions due to the fact that he is trying to find a second-hand geiger counter preparatory to summer uranium prospecting.

Up and down the footpath goes the long-suffering María Lupita, wrapped in her shabby black shawl, to tell her many troubles to Mrs. Apodaca. Up and down the footpath go Cousin Canuto's two older boys who are now in the newspaper business as carrier boys. Up and down go the five younger members of the clan headed to and from school.

"That María Lupita, *pobrecita,* she seem *muy muy cansada,* tired, these days," sighs Mrs. Apodaca. *"Ay de mí,* eet ees a hard life to have for a 'usband so great a man as my Cousin Canuto. I theenk that now all her *muchachos* are in school, maybe María Lupita weel not be so *cansada.* But she keep right on being *cansada.* She weep at every leetle theeng. She wipe the eye. She sigh. *Ay de mí,* that María Lupita ees in sad way."

After many consultations, it was decided that María Lupita should go on a long vacation. She could go back to her native village in the mountains of Rio Arriba County. The way Mrs. Apodaca spoke of it, the vacation sounded like an expedition into the dim days of early Spanish colonization.

Immediately "that Carmencita" came vociferously into the picture with the decision that María Lupita should return to her native village properly turned out. She should have a second-hand dress, coat, and hat, bought at a providential rummage sale of clothing given by the local Spanish Presbyterian church.

Mrs. Apodaca and María Lupita vetoed this innovation. Said Mrs. Apodaca, "Do you theenk

47

your Cousin Canuto's *esposa* would weesh to return to her native village feeling like a circus lady een spangles and tarlatan skirts?"

Without another word, she set about making a new black woolen dress for María Lupita. It had a full skirt that came down respectably over María Lupita's decent black cotton stockings

and over the tops of her black laced shoes. Cousin
Canuto heroically sacrificed the money he had
saved for a second-hand geiger counter to buy
María Lupita a warm black shawl and black
woolen gloves. The two boys who were in the
newspaper business bought the bus ticket and
provided a few dollars for spending money. This
money María Lupita spent in Santa Fe before
she started. She bought so many handkerchiefs

with floral borders, bars of scented soap, and pounds of hard candy to take to relatives that her purse held only her bus ticket.

At long last, a procession came down the snowy footpath beside the frozen water "deetch" and along my driveway. First came Mrs. Apodaca and María Lupita, black-skirted and black-shawled against the white background. Then came Cousin Canuto stepping elegantly along the frozen stage of my driveway. Behind him came the two older boys pushing their delivery bicycles through the white drifts. Old canvas telescope bags and innumerable boxes and bundles were fastened to the handle bars. Back of them swarmed the five youngest children carrying more of their mother's impedimenta which included a huge, flowering Christmas cactus in an old tin can. How María Lupita ever got on the bus, even with the assistance of nine people, will ever remain a mystery.

Then day by day, Mrs. Apodaca plodded along the snowy footpath up to Cousin Canuto's house to wash and iron, to clean and cook for him and the seven children. "No wonder that María Lupita ees *cansada,*" groaned Mrs. Apodaca. "Weeth all those peoples crowded into that leetle house! Coal-oil lamps to clean and feel, clothes to

50

wash and iron, food to cook and beds and beds end-to-end along every wall, even een the leetle store! 'What María Lupita need,' I say to Cousin Canuto, 'ees two more rooms and the electric wire for the lights and wash machine and water in pipe not by bucket full.' And my Cousin Canuto say, 'When I get money again for second-hand geiger counter and find my uranium mine, María Lupita shall have all these nize theengs—and more. She can seet and seet!' "

After about a month, the procession passed in return order along my snowy driveway headed for the frozen footpath beside the frozen "deetch." First came Mrs. Apodaca and María Lupita dragging their long black skirts across the sparkling whiteness. As they stopped for a moment before my window to wave and smile, I noticed with astonishment that María Lupita held in her arms a baby that looked to be about a year old. As Cousin Canuto joined them, he was leading, by a mittened hand, a little boy of about three. The two older boys pushed their bicycles along, loaded with boxes and bundles. "Every-theeng from the *ranchito,*" shouted Mrs. Apo-daca, "hand-ground blue corn meal, a *ristra* of chiles, cheekens ready to cook, dried-een-the-sun apricots and peaches."

51

Everyone was rosy and giving off little sparkles of happiness. María Lupita was *cansada* no longer. She looked about as old as Carmencita. "Those *angelitos*," she shouted, pointing to the baby in her arms and the sturdy little fellow holding Cousin Canuto's hand, "They are the *muchachos* of my brother. Now they have no mamá. I bring them home to live with us."

"Now there will be nine children in that crowded little house," I remarked later to Mrs. Apodaca. "And no electric wire for lights and washing machine. Poor María Lupita will be more *cansada* than ever."

Mrs. Apodaca shook her black-shawled head and laughed with delight. "We were all wrong, Señora. Weeth all her *muchachos* away all day een school and her 'usband busy with affairs *importantes,* she was *muy, muy solitaria*—lonely. She was not *cansada*."

JULIO VOTES DEMOCRACY

$\mathcal{B}$ack in January I started the wheels moving toward spring cleaning. This is necessary in Santa Fe if one wishes the help of Julio, the old adobe maestro. Coming home from the Plaza, walking along Chamisa Road, I saw through the murk of approaching night and falling snow, the little white dog that always precedes the maestro like a herald. In a few minutes, I almost bumped into the maestro himself. He was wearing his usual winter headgear, a knitted cap pulled down over his ears and a felt hat perched on top, matador-fashion.

"How about coming to whitewash me, Julio? Say about April first?"

"*Sí*," agreed the maestro emphatically, "I be there, Señora," and he disappeared like a ghostly matador in the swirling snow.

April first came with perfect housecleaning weather, warm sun and frolicking breezes to dry freshly whitewashed walls. But no maestro! Early on the morning of the second appeared the little white dog to be followed by Julio, his wheelbarrow filled with equipment for whatever might betide.

"Why didn't you come yesterday?" I inquired as a mere matter of form.

"Boating day (voting day)," explained the maestro in amazed tones at my stupidity.

"Of course, I voted myself. It only took a few minutes. Everyone in Santa Fe was out to vote for a mayor and new members of the City Council. How did you vote, Julio?"

"Me? I boat Democracy," explained the maestro. "I always boat Democracy."

From this I gathered that Julio had voted the straight Democratic ticket. "Why did you vote all Democracy? The other party had some good people up, too."

By this time, the maestro was stirring calsomine and water in a big pail. He stopped his professional operations long enough to explain. "Long time ago when is no jobs, my three boys have no work. The mayor of Santa Fe was *primo*, cousin, of my wife and give all my boys work.

54

That mayor was Democracy. So, of course, Señora, ever since, as long as I boat, it is right that I boat Democracy. How else can I say *Muchas gracias?*"

The situation *política* being settled, the maestro cast a professional eye at the living-room walls. "You want me to plaster-patch cracks and holes?"

Julio knows that year after year, I plaster-patch the cracks and holes myself. He looks critically at my work, shakes his head, sighs and remarks, "It is not smooze." He is right. It is not "smooze." It never is.

The maestro works steadily, singing to himself in time with the slap-slap of his whitewash brush. As he finishes one wall, I follow behind, putting up freshly laundered, yellow-print curtains, hanging pictures and restoring books to their proper places. By night, half of the little house is shining with fresh calsomine and twinkling with polished windowpanes.

When the inside of the house was as pristine as Julio and I could make it, he and the little white dog departed for the repair of outer walls while I settled down to belated work at the typewriter. All that day, I did not so much as glance at what he was doing outside. Late in the afternoon, the maestro tapped at the door. "Please come see."

I thought, of course, he wanted me to approve his work outside. But he led me to the patio wall of the house where the violinist lives. Over the smooth brown wall hung a branch from an apricot tree that grows within the patio. On that branch a few pink blossoms had opened long before the others. "Little tree," said Julio, "it send the blossoms early against the warm adobe wall." I looked at the maestro's mud-plastered hands and clothing. Again I knew why I delighted in his people. With them the emphasis is always right.

Came the day when the maestro presented his bill—all in Spanish written on a piece of old cardboard—*lunes, 8 horas; martes, 7 horas;* and so on through the days of the week. "You think it is not too much?" Julio asked anxiously as I wrote his check.

Then the grand *culminación* of each year's housecleaning! I took Julio out to the garage where there were several boxes filled with things that were not giving active service around the Little Adobe House—faded, yellow-print curtains, sweaters that had shrunk a little, pots and pans which had not earned their shelf room. "If you can take these boxes away," I suggest, "maybe someone can make use of some of the things. If they can't, let Hipólito, the trash man, cart them away."

We go through the same ceremony every year. From long experience, I know that I will see the faded curtains, freshly dyed, hanging on clotheslines in Tenorio Flat. The too-small sweaters will trot gayly through my yard on the backs of schoolward-bound *muchachos*. As for the hats and dresses, soon I will be meeting myself all over town. I have seen one of my favorite hats as far away as Chimayó perched on the modern hairdo of a señora in the village of the weavers.

The little white dog and Julio with the over-laden wheelbarrow started up the trail along the rolling hills. In a minute or two, the procession halted. Julio felt in his pocket to see if his "checkie" were safe. Then he glanced at the heaped-up treasure on the barrow. Overcome with emotion, he struggled visibly to express himself in the few English words at his command. "Señora," he shouted, "if your name is ever on boating ticket, I boat for you." But this was evidently not enough. He struggled again. "Democracy or not Democracy," he shouted.

MRS. APODACA VOTES BY LEVER

*D*uring a Presidential election year, while gardens around Santa Fe were filled with the fragrance of honeysuckle and white locust-bloom, the situation *politica* gained daily momentum among my neighbors of Tenorio Flat. Spanish Americans take as naturally to politics as tumbleweeds roll into fence corners.

As the season progressed, sedate adobe houses began to show flamboyant placards extolling the excellence of national and state candidates. "Truckies" and *carros* sported political stickers. *Rahdios* blared all day and far into the night, exhorting Tenorio Flat to vote and to vote right. Mass meetings were attended by entire families, including the babies who wept bitterly at the oratory. Laboring men in the Flat stood about in groups during the long summer evenings and talked politics. Even Grandma Segura, passing along my driveway for a day's work, wore a three-inch plastic political button affixed firmly to the front of her respectable black shawl. Mrs. Apodaca would stop and accost me with slogan *político, "Me gusta Ike."* She and Grandma Segura scarcely spoke. Grandma Segura liked another candidate.

I was therefore somewhat surprised to learn from Carmencita that the entire family and immediate neighbors were having trouble with Mamacita. Her house, their "truckie," and even her black shawl were plentifully decorated with stickers, buttons, and all the strange paraphernalia of an American election. But that was as far as Mrs. Apodaca would go. She would not vote. The husbands of Lupe, Luz and Armendita had been called in to reason with Mamacita. But she remained adamant. She refused to vote. She refused to tell why.

As usually happens during an impasse in *Casita* Apodaca, Mamacita eventually found her way to my big rocking chair and a full discussion, accompanied by glances ceilingward and dramatic gestures. After a full half-hour of preliminary amenities and a glass of chilled fruit juice, Mrs. Apodaca approached the crux of the situation by devious trails.

"Señora," she explained, "as young woman in my mountain village, I boat (vote). Was easy then. Village have head man, maybe deetch boss, maybe someone who know someone *importante* in Santa Fe, maybe an Anglo who ees like *patrón*. We do just what head man do. We use stamp to mark boating paper, and eef stamp ees lost, we use pencil that weel not rub out.

"When I marry and move to Santa Fe, ees easy to boat. We have same kind of stamp to mark boating paper. Boating ees done in front room of adobe house of neighbor. Ees all like home weeth *los muchachos* peeking een the windows. But, Señora, the last time we boat for *Presidente,* ees done een fine new school on *Acequia*. We do not have stamp or pencil to mark boating paper. They have *las máquinas de votar*—voting machines!"

Mrs. Apodaca's voice rose and quavered to a whisper. "I take one look at those great monster machines and I run away. I do not boat. How could I know eef I pool right lever or not? Better not boat at all than pool wrong lever and boat for wrong party—and *Presidente* at that!"

With her personal platform clearly defined, Mrs. Apodaca departed stiff of back and tight of lip—but complaisant of eye.

60

When election day came at last, what was my amazement to see the entire vote-eligible Apodaca family moving pollward along my driveway. Mrs. Apodaca, swathed in black from shawl-wrapped head to black cotton stockings and high kid shoes, was supported on one side by Papá Apodaca and on the other by the stalwart husband of Armendita. Behind them walked the less stalwart husbands of Lupe and Luz followed by Lupe, Luz and Armendita, themselves. Mamacita was being led protesting to the polls and her duty by a united family.

Within a few days, I learned that Mrs. Apodaca had collapsed. She cooked no food, she washed no clothes. Lupe, Luz and Armendita were forced to leave their own homes and many children to care for Mamacita and her house. "They forced her to vote with *las máquinas,* machines," laughed a neighbor, "and now she is getting even with them."

But I knew Mrs. Apodaca better than that. Something must be worrying her. Armed with her favorite delicacies, I set out and found my neighbor reclining on the couch which she had but lately painted periwinkle blue. "Oh, Señora," quavered Mrs. Apodaca, "I'm so glad you come. I must tale someone. I theenk about eet all day,

61

I theenk about eet all night. I cannot sleep. I cannot eat. I cannot tale my family. They might look at me weeth deesdain.

"Señora, Papá read to me in Spanish how to work that monster boating machine. The 'usbands of Lupe, Luz, and Armendita tale me over and over. When I go to boat, a nice lady show me all the leetle levers. Some spleet the ticket, she say, some boat straight. She pool another lever and curtains both close. I am all alone. I try to find leetle lever that say 'Ike,' but I cannot find. I look and look. Lady comes back and says through curtains, 'One hundred peoples are waiting to boat.' I get excite. I hunt and hunt for leetle lever that say, 'Ike.' The lady comes back and says, 'two hundred peoples are waiting to boat.' I pool first leetle lever I put hand on and bell rings. I have boated, but I cannot open curtains to get out. I am trapped. Lady tales me to pool beeg lever. I pool eet and I am free once more. Long line of peoples waiting to boat look at me weeth deesdain."

Mrs. Apodaca collapsed on the periwinkle-blue couch. "I know now, Señora," she groaned, "that I pool wrong lever. Please do not tale my family. They, too, would look at me weeth deesdain. *Ay de mí,* what have I deed?"

62

COUSIN CANUTO CONSIDERS
SPACE AND SHOTS

*G*limpsing several of Carmencita's space fiction *periódicos* under Cousin Canuto's arm as he strolled homeward through my yard, I became apprehensive. When Carmencita soars on the wings of a new enthusiasm, she usually lands on practical, utilitarian feet. This is not true of that hopeless romantic, her Cousin Canuto. Nearly always Cousin Canuto's flights are attended by a neglected *tiendacita,* little store, a disrupted home, and a weeping *esposa,* the long suffering María Lupita.

With some concern, I awaited the first signals of this fresh impact of Space on the receptive imagination of the volatile cousin. Usually at such times, María Lupita, swathed in a tightly-wrapped black shawl like a knight in armor, stalks through my yard for tearful conversations with an equally tearful Mrs. Apodaca. Then Mrs. Apodaca, likewise swathed in a tightly-wrapped black shawl, walks home with María Lupita. But nothing happened, nothing at all.

At last, curiosity drove me to Cousin Canuto's *placita*. It was a warm moonwashed night when earth, sky and the enfolding atmosphere seemed composed of coppertoned light. Cousin Canuto sat on his doorstep, calmly strumming his *guitarra*. María Lupita, minus her armor, sat beside him, humming a little song of her own. Out in a roof-high forest of blossoming hollyhocks, *los muchachos,* like little elves, were playing some interminable game of their own.

After the amenities had been exchanged, we sat watching the coppertoned earth and sky and listening to summer breezes purring like contented cats through the tree-lined arroyo. "Someday," I said, rallying to the purpose of my visit, "there will be space ships up there where the moon rides in a wake of copper stardust. One of *los muchachos* might even be on one."

"Perhaps," answered Cousin Canuto absently. Then, becoming aware that his lack of interest might disappoint me, he added philosophically, "If there are people up there and they do not know as much as we do, why bother them?

64

It might make them unhappy. See what Cristóbal Colón did to the poor Indians when he discovered America. If the people up in Space know more than we do, that will also take care of itself."

Cousin Canuto strummed a few more measures and then gave the contagious chuckle that usually precedes a story. "*Ay,* the poor Anglos," he sighed, "they have not learned how many times things seem to settle themselves if we have the patience to wait—big things and little things."

Cousin Canuto chuckled again. "There was *Doña* Elisa Gomez y Noriega who lived alone in the old adobe *casa* of her once-rich family. That adobe was a few miles out of town in the midst of the little piñón and cedar forests. The *sala,* drawing room, in that sagging old house had much fine old furniture: sofas, big chairs and little chairs, cushions and stools for the feet all covered with dark blue, golden brown, and purple plush. The outside door to the *sala* had many little panes of glass. One of these panes of glass became broken and fell out. *Doña* Elisa did not hurry to have the broken glass replaced. The hole in the door remained.

"It remained when she packed her little tin trunk and went far down the Rio Grande to visit some *primos,* cousins, for a month or more. When she returned, she was unhappy to find her fine furniture covered with the hair of many cats who had come in through the hole in her door. In the cold snowy weather, they had used her *sala* as a cat hotel. Yellow hair, black hair, white hair and brindle hair was all over her fine plush furniture. *Doña* Elisa tried to brush off that hair, but there was so much of it and it clung so tight to the plush that she decided to leave it for awhile until she rested from her long trip.

"So she rested for many weeks until she received another warm invitation to visit other *primos* in Tierra Amarilla. Again she packed her little tin trunk and departed for the Valley of the Cousins. Behind her, the hole in the door remained unmended and cat hairs still clung to the fine plush furniture of her ancestors. At the end of another month of *primo*-visiting, *Doña* Elisa returned to the raveling adobe of her ancestors. Unhappily she thought that now she must hire someone out of her scanty *dinero* to mend her front door and take the cat hairs from her fine plush furniture.

"But when she went into the *sala,* she could not believe her eyes. There was no cat hair left on the fine plush sofas and chairs—not one. Then came a scurry of a little animal across the sagging floor boards. As it scampered through the glass-less hole in the door, from its crammed mouth projected the last of the cat hairs gleaned from the sofas and chairs. 'Ah,' exclaimed the gentle *Doña* Elisa when she told me the story, 'How warm have the baby trader-rats slept this cold, late spring because of nests lined with cat hair garnered from the fine plush furniture of my ancestors.' "

Cousin Canuto strummed his *guitarra* softly, *los muchachos* came and put their sleepy heads in their mamacita's capacious lap. The big moon moved steadily on through limitless space. Mesas and mountains lost their metallic color-tones and turned to softest velvet.

"Should a man from Space land in New Mexico, I know what would amaze him the most," exclaimed Cousin Canuto, "that is if he lands in the season of *turistas*—tourists. Just imagine, Señora, a man from another world confronted with hundreds of people in cars and on foot, advancing like little soldiers on our old town of Santa Fe. But these soldiers do not carry guns. Each one carries a little machine for taking pictures in a fine leather case slung across his shoulders. In other fine leather cases are devices to measure light, bulbs that flare up in dark corners and more film to take pictures.

"And every *turista,* laden like a burrito with all these fine leather cases, goes prowling around with a look of great concern and intensity on the face. Ah, Señora, the taking of pictures now is a matter of great solemnity. When one *turista* starts to take a picture, up rush other picture-takers. There are prolonged consultations which result in everyone changing the distance or the light or something over and over again. They might be splitting the atom instead of taking a picture of something beautiful.

"*Ay de mí,* when the man from Space learns a little Spanish, he will ask, 'What are they doing, Canuto?' And I will answer, 'Taking pictures.' 'Haven't they eyes and minds and hearts to remember the beautiful things they see?' the man from Space will ask."

"Nonsense." I rushed to the defense of picture-takers. "With fast transportation by plane and car, *turistas* see more wonders in a few days of vacation now than they did in months a few years ago. Seeing so much in a short time, pictures bring back to the memory the scenes that delighted the eyes and minds and hearts. And besides, many people cannot get away to travel about the country and they like to see the pictures travelers have taken."

68

"*Si*," agreed Cousin Canuto tolerantly, "I have nothing against picture-taking people, but I wish they could do it with less solemnity. I guided one carload of four picture-takers all around Santa Fe last summer. They were very nice people. They said they wanted me to guide them to some outstanding shots. That is what they call taking a picture, Señora. It is a word not pleasant on the ear to my way of thinking."

Cousin Canuto's eyes twinkled. "We had some very funny times. I still laugh to think of them. You know, Señora, the fine adobe home of a famous sculptor on that road near the mountains? A high adobe wall is in front of the house, but at one side where the wall does not reach, are heaps and piles of things the sculptor has collected to use when he builds more rooms as he plans to do. There are great stacks of old carved doors, old window frames, heaps of broken adobe bricks, lumber and *vigas* from old houses that have been torn down.

"The picture-taking señor saw all this and stopped the car. Before I knew why he had stopped, he was pulling the rope at the gateway in the adobe wall. A big bell that the sculptor had bought from an old church tolled mournfully in the house. In a few minutes the lady of the house opened the door in the gateway. 'Please,' said the shot-taking señor, 'may I come in and take a shot of the fine old ruins?'

"The lady of the house stood up very straight in her hand-carved gateway. 'This is my home,' she said, very red of face and stiff of back. 'Not an old ruin.' She closed the door with quite a bang and bolted it from the inside.

" 'Well,' exclaimed the shot-taking señor, 'I thought everyone around Santa Fe just doted on old ruins!' "

Cousin Canuto laughed so hard over this that he had to mop his eyes with a red bandanna. "The next day, these same people asked me to guide them to some places where they could get shots of fine scenery. I took them over Pecos way and up into the mountains where the road ends and the wilderness begins. Señora, you know how that country is in summer—untouched forests of pine topped by blue spruce like a silver picture frame. Mountain streams tumbling down from melting snow and spreading out to sing and glitter under the alder trees. Wild cosmos dancing in the breezes. Banks of white and purple violets and clumps of red and the yellow columbine. Those picture-taking people got out all their picture-taking devices. They consult and

70

they argue and they look very, very serious and they take shots and shots. They use up all their films.

"On the way home where the road goes over a high ridge, out across the valley where a sudden shower had passed, hung the finest, brightest double rainbow I had ever seen. 'Look, look,' I cried, 'a double rainbow, the best I have ever seen.'

"The shot-taking señor stopped the car for one little minute and looked where I pointed. Then he shook his head. 'No use,' he groaned, 'not one bit of film left in the crowd.' Without one look behind, he continued on down the valley of the Pecos."

Cousin Canuto seemed quite overcome by this experience. But at last he asked, "What is the best thing you have ever seen to make a picture, Señora?"

I thought of caribou coming down to drink of the icy waters of the Yukon rolling through untouched forests. I thought of the day "Popo" emerged from the mists that floated over Mexico City. I thought of silver-backed leaves in the rain forests of the Caribbean islands. Then I laughed.

"The most beautiful subject for a picture that I ever saw is not far away from here. I see it every winter. Rosy, thick-walled little adobe houses climbing the snowy hill back of my place. Each house has a prim ruching of snow along its fire wall and a giddy feather of smoke flaunting from its squat black chimney. Over all is a blue, snow-scoured sky and a golden paten of sun. And the great blue mountains spread their white glistening wings as if they were trying to reach that golden paten."

"Did you ever take a picture of it?" demanded Cousin Canuto.

"Of course not," I gasped. "It is part of me."

Cousin Canuto leaped happily to his feet. "The camera of the heart," he exulted, "never runs out of film."

SERGEANT SEGURA'S RETURN

*S*eñor and Señora Segura live in the most amusing little adobe house in all Tenorio Flat. Necessity fashioned it from odds and ends as their family had increased.

Now that their five sons had left them and scattered over the region for adobes of their own, the Seguras clung the more tightly to their strangely-angled, out-of-line little home. Only their youngest son had not married. He was in the army of the U Esse. His parents, in speaking of him, always gave him his full military title of Sergeant Segura.

Although they had no daughters, the Seguras were *padrinos,* godparents, to the daughter of a friend and they always referred to her as Little Teresa of Tucumcari. In their eyes, she was everything that was good, capable and beautiful. Since she had reached the age of twenty, they were beginning to worry why she did not marry.

In spite of their many years, Señor and Señora Segura asked nothing of anyone, not even of their stalwart sons. They owned their funny little house. The Señor kept a goat and a few "cheekens." They had no utility bills to pay. Water came from a blue-hooded well. The Señora kept two glass lamps twinkling like stars. Piñón wood in a big iron cookstove both heated and perfumed their snug little home.

As for the small amount of money needed, the Señor and Señora had worked out a unique system of cooperation. When the weather became pleasant in early spring, Señora Segura took just enough days of housework in an Anglo family to cover their modest needs. From lilac time to aspen gold, she trotted happily through my yard bent on earning enough *dinero* for groceries, a new dress or two and even an occasional present for Little Teresa of Tucumcari. During these pleasant days, Señor Segura puttered about the goat corral, munched piñón nuts in the Plaza with a *compadre,* and rested and rested.

But when the wintry winds war-whooped through high mountain passes in November, Señor Segura donned his sheepskin coat and red muffler and took a job as night watchman. Then Señora Segura puttered with her geranium plants in sunny windows, cooked the best highly-seasoned viands in the region, and rested and rested. It was her turn now.

All was going happily until Sergeant Segura completed his turn with the U Esse Army. He was scarcely back in blue jeans before he took things in his own masterful hands. His papá and mamacita had worked long enough. From now on they should both rest the whole year long. To substantiate his words, he found work with a plumbing company at good wages. All Tenorio Flat beamed with approval of Sergeant Segura. He was a noble young man who would take proper care of his parents who had many years.

But in a month or two, Sergeant Segura was looking with disdain at the ancestral adobe—no bathtub, no piped water, no gas stove, no electricity. Being a man of action fresh from the army of the U Esse, he acted with speed and decision. Across town in a new real-estate subdivision, he bought—on contract—a new house. It had everything, piped water, a bathtub, gas range, and electricity. He bought—also on contract—suitable furnishings for the jerry-built house—shining brass beds, sofa and chairs upholstered in red brocade and a dinette suite which threatened to collapse at any minute. Sergeant Segura was now neatly buried under monthly payments right up to his happy eyes.

The goat was sold, the "cheekens" were consumed, and the Segura family departed for a life of elegance with continual rest for the elders and consequent happiness. The amusing adobe with all its contents was put up for sale. But no one wanted an amusing adobe sans plumbing.

Every week or two Señor and Señora returned to look at their deserted little house. Señora Segura blackened and polished the old wood-burning cookstove and her tears fell on its highly polished surface. Señor Segura swept the hard-packed patina of his adobe yard and kept his eyes resolutely turned away from the goat corral and the pen for the "cheekens." For the first time I realized that Señor and Señora Segura must have been very, very elderly when they lived among us. No wonder Sergeant Segura had acted with such decision!

Then one blustering November night, I noticed a feather of piñón smoke floating from the crooked chimney of the Segura adobe. I dashed over at top speed to protect the property of my one-time neighbors from possible harm.

None was in sight. Señora Segura was frying blue corn *tortillas* and stirring *frijoles* in a big brown pot. With a white flour sack bound about her head, she looked positively bridelike. "Sergeant Segura could not sell our home," she explained. "We had to move back to take care of it. You know how an empty house can go to pieces!"

Out of the tiny bedroom strode Señor Segura as nimbly as a lad. He was wearing his sheepskin coat and red muffler. "I have to get to my night watchman job," he said gayly. "It's the best one I ever had and ten cents more an hour. Next payday I buy some cheekens, but alas, no goat. There is a new law that we cannot keep livestock in the city limits. What will they think up next?"

After his triumphant departure, Señora Segura and I ate blue corn *tortillas* spread with wild-plum jelly. "Poor, poor Sergeant Segura," I worried. "No one to keep his new house for him! And buried under monthly payments for years without end!"

Señora Segura twinkled with happiness. "He will have help, good help with everything—the house, the cooking, the payments."

"But how?" I questioned.

"Little Teresa of Tucumcari," whispered Señora Segura, as radiant as a bride herself.

NOBLE SERGEANT SEGURA

*N*o one in all Santa Fe's Tenorio Flat ever reveled in a crooked-walled little adobe house more than Señor and Señora Segura. Their escape from enforced idleness in the modern, jerry-built home of their son, Sergeant Segura, simply gilded their days with delight.

Señor and Señora Segura were no happier than was Tenorio Flat to have them back. When their wedding *aniversario* came in early January, the Flat observed it with abandon. For days, little girls stepping cautiously, carried white-covered plates and platters to the Segura's sagging front door. Little boys, grinning and trying to appear nonchalant, carried wrapped parcels and pots of blooming geraniums. "Mamacita sent this to you. She *wants* you to have it."

Married sons with their families drove in from the country in horse-drawn wagons or "truckies" and deposited piñón wood, dried apricots, peaches, beans, chile and blue corn ground in a hand mill. The long dining table covered with roseate oilcloth was heaped all day with a never-failing bounty of highly seasoned, savory food. People came and went continuously—all Tenorio Flat, *primos* and *compadres* from as far away as Truchas and Trampas. No one was missing, no one at all—but Sergeant Segura and his wife, Little Teresa of Tucumcari.

But Tenorio Flat knew that Sergeant Segura, that estimable young man who had tried to give his parents the ease and luxury their many years deserved, ah, Sergeant Segura would not forget his papá and mamacita on their *aniversario*. In spite of the unhappy evidence, Tenorio Flat to a man remained loyal to Sergeant Segura.

It was well they did. The very next morning, the Sunday calm of Tenorio Flat was broken by a bright-blue car containing the Sergeant and Little Teresa. With horn-tooting and laughter they drove to the paternal adobe. In the twinkling of an eye, the Sergeant was seen to emerge with his mamacita wrapped in her best shawl and his papá muffled to the ears in his sheepskin coat. It was reported that they went down the highway as far as Pecos where they dined in great elegance in an Anglo cafe on fried chicken and apple pie topped with ice cream.

When they returned, Tenorio Flat came over in discreet relays to inspect the Sergeant's new *automóvil*. It was not a new *automóvil*. In fact, it had served various owners for some twelve years. But it looked new, with its bright-blue paint and seatcovers of crimson plastic. Men raised the hood and listened to the motor and nodded approving heads. *Muchachos* tooted the horn and pretended to steer. Señoras patted the seatcovers and rolled admiring eyes heavenward. "Ah, what a son is Sergeant Segura to take his parents for an *aniversario* ride in his fine new *automóvil!*"

At last, dramatically, Sergeant Segura closed the car windows, locked the doors and handed the keys to his papá, the while enfolding him in a filial embrace. Little Teresa kissed mamacita on either cheek. Then laughing and looking backward with much waving of hands, they started to walk the two miles to their own home across town. Tenorio Flat stood breathless with emotion at sight of the drama enacted before their eyes. The fine new car no longer belonged to Sergeant Segura. He had given it to his parents for an *aniversario* present. It was time for tears and a time for laughter. Tenorio Flat indulged in both.

Señor Segura built a little *ramada* of pine tree saplings over the precious car. He thatched its top and sides with piñón branches closely woven. Every day he wiped the car's high polish with a piece of lamb's wool. Every day the Señora polished the windshield and windows until they twinkled like diamonds. There that marvel of an *automóvil* stood through weeks and weeks. It stood like some rare exhibit in an evergreen shrine. For neither Señor nor Señora Segura could drive a car and would never learn to do so. It was enough just to polish and admire it and to wait for the far-apart days when their son could pilot them down the highway.

Early in February, Señora Segura started working regularly four days a week in an Anglo house. This was the time of year when she always stayed snugly under cover. At that, a troublesome thought kept returning to me. I knew that Sergeant Segura was plastered with monthly payments right up to his noble eyebrows—payments on his house, his furniture, his electrical equipment, and even on his wedding clothing. It was taking all he and Little Teresa could both earn to keep their heads above the tidal wave of payments. Without a doubt, the *aniversario auto-*

móvil had likewise been purchased on monthly payments. And now mamacita was working entirely off schedule to help meet those payments.

One night when Cousin Canuto and I were talking before the corner fireplace, I voiced my suppositions. Cousin Canuto looked at me as if I had voiced heresy, sedition, and revolution. "That *automóvil* was a gift, Señora. A gift is like an iceberg. Only a little part of the gift can you see and touch. The biggest part and the best part of a gift is the love that prompted it. So you cannot pay for a gift."

I sat properly rebuked until Cousin Canuto lifted a quizzical eyebrow. "There is, of course, no reason why the parents of Sergeant Segura should not make him a present in return. That would not be against politeness. I happen to know that Señora Segura has now made him a present of a final payment on his dinette suite. Next month she will start on the overstuffed sofa and in time, make him a present of that. Señor Segura is going to get some garden work this summer and pay off the Sergeant's *rahdio* and make a start on the electric refrigerator—as gifts, of course."

Cousin Canuto laughed with delight. "Before they get through," he chuckled, "no one will know who gave anyone what."

"MEES" BOGGERS
AND THE BEAUTIFUL WAY

A few nights before Christmas, Mrs. Apodaca came to sit before my corner fireplace. By light from the flame and twinkle of tall turquoise candles in the greenery-hung little room, I could see that my neighbor was in a dramatic mood. She was wearing a new black dress with a full, long skirt. Her high laced shoes glowed with polish. As she leaned back in the big rocker, two inches of new black cotton stocking came elegantly into sight. Her big, old-fashioned gold-loop earrings seemed made of flame, so brilliant was their luster. "Señora," she announced, "I am walking the beautiful way of Creesmas!"

Where, I wondered, had Mrs. Apodaca picked up the expression, "walking the beautiful way"? It was not part of her Spanish heritage. It was indeed, straight Indian, and Navajo Indian at that. I might have known that "Mees" Boggers would figure dramatically in its acquisition.

After a long period of silent contemplation, Mrs. Apodaca burst out, "Mees Emily, the Anglo lady who has many friends among *los indios*, took Mees Boggers to the land of the Nabahoos in *octubre*. They rented a Nabahoo house that had a board floor and two old wire cots and a rusted iron stove that have only three legs. They take along many warm blankets and boxes of much good food."

Mrs. Apodaca mused for a good ten minutes over this setting for her drama. The piñón fire purred. So did that estimable feline, El Hijo de Koshare. So did Mrs. Apodaca—figuratively speaking.

"Mees Emily take Mees Boggers," she continued, "to see some of her Nabahoo friends. The Nabahoo lady at one place show them a rug she has woven. Never ees a rug like that, say Mees Boggers, since old, old days. The Nabahoo lady had spun the yarn from wool of her own sheep and dyed it weeth juniper bark and yellow chamisa and flowers from the bee plant. The Nabahoo lady say she hear by Nabahoo grapevine that the trader at Falling Mountain Trading Post have

84

reech man in *Nueva* York who would pay beeg price for a rug like that, but the trading post ees far, far away.

"So," said Mrs. Apodaca, plunging with zest into the drama, "the Nabahoo lady make hot drink for visitors from the leaves of a boosh that grow in Nabahoo land. Mees Boggers like that drink very much. She say it taste of all good things that blow in the air of Nabahoo land—sunshine and sagebrush and flowers of the desert."

Mrs. Apodaca's eyes twinkled and she covered a smile politely with a small hand. "You know, Señora, how Mees Boggers ees—a leetle like a pack rat. She collects theengs. So when she get a chance, she wheesper to Mees Emily, 'See if we can get her to go weeth us in the car to where that leetle boosh grow weeth leaves for good drink.' And the Nabahoo lady say she weel do and they weel go far, far away. And Mees Emily say, 'Good' and they weel make peekneek next day, and they hurry back to their Nabahoo house to cook much food for peekneek.

"It ees good they do, Señora. Next morning, not only Nabahoo lady, but Nabahoo man and lots of Nabahoo children and even a Nabahoo baby on cradleboard crowd into that car. And they drive and they drive over what looks like no

85

road at all. But the Nabahoo man know the way. Mees Boggers tale me, not even in lands across *el océano* did she ever see such beeg beautiful *montañas* and such bright, bright color.

"About noon they come to old trading post and Nabahoo lady get out weeth beeg bundle and baby on cradleboard. She ees gone long, long time, but at last she come out weeth smiles on face and much *dinero* in both hands.

"So they make peekneek near trading post and all around grow booshes that have leaves Mees Boggers want. The Nabahoo family peek and peek and soon they have plenty even for Mees Boggers. On the way home Mees Boggers say the sun shine so that *las montañas* look like beeg balloons floating up, up into the sky and all the beeg high cleefs are as red as Chimayó chiles. Right in the meedle of all this, down the yellow sand road come walking a Nabahoo of many years and he ask the car to stop and he say to Nabahoo man in car, 'Are you walking the Beautiful Way?' And the Nabahoo man in car say, 'Yes, we are walking the Beautiful Way.' "

Mrs. Apodaca was evidently approaching the climax to her drama, as she was gesticulating with her brown index finger on which glittered the big silver ring with the turquoise setting.

"Wheen they let the Nabahoo family out at their house, Mees Emily say they been over two hundred miles. And wheen Mees Boggers get out at their house, she give beeg scream. All around that house, Señora, grow booshes weeth leaves they had gone two hundred miles to find. She run into house and shout, 'Eet ees not nice of that Nabahoo lady to make us drive two hundred miles over bad road to sell her rug when she know those booshes grow almost in our house.'

"But Mees Emily ees seeting on old wire cot seenging about Walking the Beautiful Way in a song the Nabahoos have. 'Eet ees finish een beauty,' she seeng and that ees all the answer she geeve Mees Boggers. All the way back to Santa Fe, wheen Mees Boggers sputter about Nabahoo lady, Mees Emily seeng, 'Eet ees finished in beauty,' over and over again."

Mrs. Apodaca paused so long that I thought this last drama of "Mees" Boggers had come to a grand finale, but at length she produced the last scene. "One day I work for Mees Boggers and in come Mees Emily. Right away Mees Boggers say, 'I can still see those booshes right in front of our Nabahoo house.'

"Mees Emily say, 'Eudora, do you know what a Nabahoo winter is like, all shut in by deep snow and no work for man and all those children to feed? Every time I theenk of all the sacks of flour and cans of lard and milk all that money from the fine rug would buy, I shout for joy. As for us, we see Nabahoo country few but Nabahoos ever see. We hear Nabahoo man give ancient greeting. Walking the Beautiful Way mean more than just seeing beautiful country.'

"And Mees Boggers wipe tears from eyes and say, 'How you theenk I can get nize Creesmas box to that Nabahoo family?''

Mrs. Apodaca drew her shawl over her head and walked her own beautiful way homeward under the stars of "Creesmas."

WINTRY DANCE PLAZAS

*I*n New Mexico's Rio Grande pueblos, Indians dance between Christmas and the New Year. The place, the date, the hour and kind of ancient ceremonial to be given are largely a matter of vague hearsay. Wrapped warmly against the cold, one starts out early in the morning and drives from pueblo to pueblo. Somewhere along this old river of murky water and scintillant history, one will hear the roar of *tombés,* the hiss of rattle-gourds, the pat of dancing feet and will be submerged in color, rhythm, and a sense of things primeval.

During an unhurried day we visited four pueblos. At two we found dances and at two others we found something almost as good—Indians going about their own way of life unbeset by crowds of curious non-Indians.

As we approached Santo Domingo Pueblo,

89

far down the winding road that leads from the highway, we could hear the roar of drums pounding like surf against the shore. No snow had fallen and the packed adobe of the long dance plaza reflected the wintry lights and shadows of surrounding ruddy hills and color-flooded mesa heights. Sun poured down from a winter-blue sky, but a bitter wind sang along the kiva tops and over flat-roofed thick-walled houses standing side by side around the plaza.

These low adobe houses, weathered by the centuries, held within the dance plaza a fragrant atmosphere of cedar smoke curling from many blackened chimneys. At either end, stark ladders from kiva depths reached for the winter sky. Blanket-wrapped men and women sat along the roof tops or on benches along their weathered *portales*. They gave us welcoming smiles and pointed to empty seats on the benches. But there is something about an Indian dance that is hard for me to take sitting down. I want the full impact from my toes to the crown of my head.

Out of the kiva came four blanket-wrapped drummers pounding waist-high ceremonial drums. After them came blanketed chanters—old men and young men voicing the ancient monosyllabic words. In spite of the blankets that wrapped them from head to knees, I recognized several Indians I had seen around Santa Fe—artists, craftsmen, young moderns holding jobs in stores and offices.

Shepherded by Koshares with dried corn-husks in their hair, came a long line of children from the kiva. The little boys wore richly embroidered dance kilts. Their painted torsos were crossed by bands of seashells. Parrot feathers, wired to modern haircuts, bobbed as they danced. In one hand each held a sprig of evergreen, the symbol of everlasting life, and in the other an ever-active rattle that had caught the rhythm of the roaring drums. Little girls wore gay kirtles and on their heads were wooden *tablitas* representing mesas decorated with the symbols of rain and snow. They carried evergreen twigs in both hands and did most of their dancing with stiff, oriental movements of their arms and hands.

Many people in New Mexico remark, "Better see all the Indian dances you can. Someday there will be no more." But I saw probably two hundred Indian children of Santo Domingo dancing the ancient steps. Their ages ranged from about eleven to toddlers who knew the steps but were continually leaving the lines to put on little shows of their own. Their elders sat smiling

91

and at ease while their children danced on the
wintry plaza filled with the lights and shadows
filtering down from the blue hulk of Jémez
Mountain.

Santa Clara and San Ildefonso pueblos farther up the Rio Grande showed no signs of dancing along their wind-swept plazas. But it was good
just to be in the house-rimmed squares, which

92

held the scent of cedar fires and to see the kiva ladders here also reaching starkly for the illimitable sky.

Little Tesuque Pueblo, which we passed on our way home almost at dusk, also seemed devoid of dancing feet. Men huddled together and talked in sheltered corners. Women went on neighborly visits from house to house. Children showed their new dolls and bats and balls. The west was showing brown and copper lights against the glow of a winter sunset. Wind blew over the dance plaza as if it had come from some primeval polar icecap. Cold and a little disappointed, we drove out on the windy plaza to turn the car about and retreat to our snug adobes and blazing corner fireplaces.

But out on that night-filling plaza we almost collided with dancers emerging from the kiva. There on that wind-swept square in the bronze-colored light of fading day they gave one of the most beautiful animal dances I had ever seen. The women wore hand-woven kirtles exquisitely embroidered in rose, turquoise and black. The men dancers who took the parts of buffalos wore the shaggy heads of the "hunchbacked cattle" over their own. Other men dancers who represented deer had deer antlers fastened to their heads and leaned on little canes in their hands to represent the appearance of quadrupeds. Two little boys played the part of fawns, and there were two dancers who had the great curved horns of the mountain sheep fastened to their heads.

With great precision the dancers of Tesuque gave their ancient winter dance of the animals, the buffalo of the great plains, the deer of the dark forests, and the mountain sheep of the rocky heights. There in a small pueblo not far from Santa Fe where Indian homes know the use of electricity for radios, lighting, and refrigeration, the people danced to perfection the ceremonial of their ancients with the light of a waning winter's day illuminating their authentic costumes and exact steps.

There is an old Athabascan saying which states that he who sees well in winter light will walk with beauty when spring comes. Perhaps, in these days of rapid adjustment to modern times, all Indians are walking in winter light. They will not have to wait for spring to walk with beauty. They have that in their hearts.

GREAT-GRANDMOTHER'S
TWO WORDS

$\mathcal{F}$or many years "Mees" Emily has known an Indian family of three generations in a pueblo near Santa Fe. When a fourth generation appeared, a great feast was prepared and "Mees" Emily and I, the only non-Indians, were invited. "We feed the people" was the way a younger generation described the festivities.

As we rolled pueblo-ward in the shadow of blue mesa tops, "Mees" Emily reminded me that I had seen members of the family dancing in winter Deer Dances and in summer Corn Dances. They were modern Indians who still performed all of their kiva duties. "When you meet Great-Grandmother," she urged, "see if you don't think she has the most beautiful face you ever saw."

The family lived close to the floor-smooth ancient dance plaza. Their house was adobe, like our own. Sturdy ranchstyle couches and chairs were filled with visiting Indians. The fourth generation slept in a modern white bassinet with pink silk lining and coverlet.

In the adjoining room was a long dining table with chairs at the ends and long benches down the sides. From time to time, "the people" were summoned in orderly relays to that great table—"Mees" Emily and I among them. This was no mid-afternoon collation. There were great loaves of whole-wheat bread baked in the beehive-shaped out-door ovens, *chile con carne* in enormous bowls, wild-plum jam, great brown-crusted prune pies, cakes, fruit and candy.

Indian visitors of all ages came into the living room, admired the little boy in his pink-and-white bassinet, settled themselves in chairs and exchanged pueblo news in low voices, then took their turns at the long table and left to make room for others.

But "Mees" Emily and I did not make the customary exit. We sat and sat because "Mees" Emily wanted me to see Great-Grandmother and she had not appeared. At last, in desperation, she probably broke all Indian social usage and asked a young man member of the family where Great-Grandmother might be.

The young Indian laughed heartily and explained, "She won't be along until late afternoon. Our pueblo is playing baseball against Cochiti a little way down the road. Great-Grandmother has gone to the ball game and I know she won't leave until the last ball has been pitched."

Fresh relays of visitors came to admire the baby, shook hands with the young parents, disappeared around the corner into the dining room and made unhurried exits. Children played in the yard and came in at short intervals for more and more food. Processions of Indians came and went. "Mees" Emily and I glanced anxiously at each other. We were probably staying far beyond Indian decorum.

Almost at nightfall, a truck rattled up and stopped with a shriek of brakes. Out hopped a little old lady as easily as a girl. Half the roomful rushed out to greet her. Came laughter and excited conversation in Tewa. It seemed Cochiti's ball team had won after all. But Great-Grandmother had hoped until the end.

"Mees" Emily and I joined the others greeting Great-Grandmother in the yard. "She doesn't speak or understand much English," whispered

"Mees" Emily. "Shake hands gently, Indian style, the way I've taught you."

Great-Grandmother, a slip of a woman, was dressed in the ancient costume, the *manta,* a black, sliplike dress fastened on the right shoulder and going under the left arm. A black shawl crossed her shoulders. From the black background of *manta* and shawl came the glitter of exquisite silver and turquoise jewelry. White hair pulled back into a neckline coil made a frame for a face such as I had never seen, a dark face lighted by great eyes which had looked on much living and found it good.

When "Mees" Emily introduced me, I remembered the gentle palm-to-palm touch of an Indian handshake. Great-Grandmother beamed. "Thank you," she said in a soft voice. I was to learn afterward that those two words were all the English she knew.

The last of the Indian visitors disappeared homeward. The young mother wheeled the bassinet into another room to settle the much-admired baby for a night's sleep. "Mees" Emily and the family wandered away to inspect a new room where modern plumbing was to be installed. Great-Grandmother settled herself on a couch and beckoned me to sit beside her.

We must have sat thus alone for almost an hour. From time to time, Great-Grandmother would touch my hand gently like the flick of a butterfly wing. Then she would turn and look earnestly into my face and say, "Thank you."

"Thank you," I would reply. It seemed a most satisfactory conversation.

When "Mees" Emily returned from prolonged inspection of a new bathroom, she stood a long time in the doorway looking at Great-Grandmother and me. "Neither one of you looks as if you had a bone in your body," she exclaimed. "You look so relaxed."

On the way home, between the little Indian houses where fragrant supper fires were burning in the still night air, "Mees" Emily laughed. "I never saw two people enjoying each other so much with only two words of a common tongue between them."

"When I came out here this afternoon," I confessed, "I felt as if I couldn't make it. It had been one of those weeks. But now I'm as rested as if I had spent the day on some mountaintop. What does Great-Grandmother have that needs no words in any language?"

"Mees" Emily laughed and touched my hand. "Thank you," she whispered.

𝒥ust as the old adobe maestro, Julio, is custodian of walls within and without the Little Adobe House, so Prudencio is custodian of roofs and the more complicated procedures involving carpentry. Although much younger, Prudencio is also an old-time craftsman. This is evidenced by an ability, even a compulsion to "make do."

A handful of nails, ends of lumber, a yard of tarpaper, a little paint in the bottom of a can— all are carefully put away for future use. After years of such hoarding, my garage has become a New Mexican version of The Old Curiosity Shop. If either workman has to order any new materials, he does so with unhappy reluctance.

When I bought the Little Adobe House many years ago, it had a long narrow kitchen with a blank wall on one side, and shelves, drainboard, and stove along another, equally blank. The only light it received came from an adjoining room. Like Julio and Prudencio, I "made do" for years.

That long, blank outer wall held one break in its thick white contour. The previous owner evidently had a great liking for parts of old iron stoves. Into that wall she had inserted the iron doors of a big black heating stove. They opened and closed ponderously over a four-inch indenture in the wall. Everyone who entered my kitchen would exclaim, "What is that?" If the inquirers were men they would roar with laughter when I answered, "It is my tool box." When they opened the massive black iron doors and saw my dime-store equipment—tacks, small nails, a fragile hammer, screw driver, and gimlet—they usually went into hysterics.

At last I determined to remove that ridiculous tool chest imbedded in hard adobe mortar if I had to knock down the wall that held it. Why not do better than that? Why not fill in that wall space with all the little square-paned windows it would take? By dint of careful measuring with my sewing-basket tape measure, it seemed that I might have six feet of window glass over a yard high facing the southern sky.

Prudencio, summoned by postcard as he has no *teléfono,* appeared in a month's time. His hat was on the back of his head and he twinkled with anticipation. He, too, measured, but with a steel tape. Windows were possible! Then he searched the garage for "make do" materials.

He would need to buy no nails, but a couple of "heenges." It would take three new window casements set side by side to fill the six-foot space and two lintels of thick, strong lumber. Everything else we had—boards, screening, putty, and turquoise paint.

The next morning Prudencio and his papá arrived to start the grand enterprise. Papá, it seemed, was an expert on windows—especially lintels. After papá's inspection, Prudencio appeared before me in dismay. "My papá say that with the weight of four heavy *begas*, ceiling beams, on that wall, we will have to prop up the two end *begas* when we knock out the adobe bricks. We need two long two-by-fours for props because if those *begas* slip, the roof on that side of the house will cave in and then where will we be? And I can't find any two-by-fours long enough."

"Ask the Big Jo Lumber Company to rush us up a couple of two-by-fours just the length you need," I suggested.

Prudencio hesitated at the thought of such additional expense. "I look once more in garage."

He came back smiling. "You know that long ladder we use when we fix roof when she leak? That ladder has side pieces made of long two-by-fours. I'll just knock off the crosspieces and nail them back on when we're through with using the sides to prop up the *begas*."

The ladder two-by-fours were soon propped under each end *bega*. Papá, armed with a short-handled pick went outside to make an opening in the thick wall for the lintels. Prudencio picked from the inside. He no longer sang. Grain by grain they picked. Papá came inside the Little Adobe House at five-minute intervals to see if the end *begas* were slipping. "It's dangerous," he warned me. "One little slip and the roof caves in." I sat at a safe distance and felt like a mariner riding out a gale and wondering if the anchors would hold.

At last, a thread of blue atmosphere showed along the top of the wall. It grew wider and wider. Prudencio dashed outside. Came the sound of heavy wood sliding inch by inch along rough adobe. Then both men stood before me. "The danger is all over," they exclaimed exultantly. "The outside lintel is in place. Now we'll slip the inside lintel in beside it and then we can work fast."

103

And fast they worked—hacking out the thick adobe bricks carefully. They must not be broken. They must be saved. Prudencio sang happily in Spanish. Papá whistled and hummed. By noon the wall was ready for the casements and I owned a big segment of blue New Mexican sky. I owned a flood of golden sunlight and the black trunk of the white-flowering locust tree and the lovely *portál* and garden of the Old Rock House next door.

By night the windows were in place, set up in fresh adobe mortar. The woodwork was complete and painted turquoise blue like the sky. As the men were leaving, Prudencio hesitated in embarrassment. "We nail the crosspieces back on the two-by-fours of your ladder, Señora. It is all right, only it won't be as long as it used to be. You see we had to saw off quite a lot from each two-by-four to make them fit under those *begas,* so the *begas* won't slip and the roof cave in. Come and see, Señora."

Out in the garage, the ladder that used to reach to the roof top, was now quite a stubby affair. At least two feet had been sawed off to "make do" as two-by-fours. "Poor little ladder," sighed Prudencio, looking at it, "maybe I make mistake."

104

"*Demasiado*—too much 'make do.' " I chuckled.

"What you mean, poor little ladder?" asked Papá smiling benignly. "Fine little ladder, it brings the sun and the moon and the stars right into the Señora's kitchen. Can a lady have more than that? *¡Verdad!*"

A BOOK
IN AN OLD IRON SAFE

Questing for and acquiring native workmen to make the necessary repairs and improvements is one of the chief joys of living in a little adobe house. During the first few years I experimented with Anglo workmen. It was about as successful as asking a drum and cymbal player to coax melody from a harpsichord. Native workmen accept the whimsicalities of little adobe houses with respect, understanding, and a reciprocal gaiety.

Almost as soon as I moved into the Little Adobe House, I acquired Julio, the old adobe maestro who speaks little English. In time, I acquired Prudencio for carpentry and roof work. He is about the age of Julio's middle-aged "boys." He speaks English quite freely, but with an amusing intonation that sometimes leads me astray.

But for all his modernity, he remains a native workman with great ability to "make do." "I theenk it will work," he always says in some perplexing repair situation. "I hope so." It always does!

It is only within the last few years that I have acquired a native plumber. He is about the age of Prudencio, but he speaks English well, has evidently been through high school and is the proud possessor of a city plumbing license. It is evidence of my fearful respect for all plumbers and their bills that I never call him by his first name as I do Julio and Prudencio. He is always Mr. Sandoval to me. He does not sing in English nor in Spanish as he works as do the other two. Nevertheless, there remains with Mr. Sandoval a native light-hearted and reassuring manner with plumbing problems.

He is the only one of the three who has a telephone. I walk to Julio's small adobe when I need his help. As Prudencio lives across town, I keep on my desk a stack of post cards which I call "Prudencio cards," to summon him when I need his particular skills. If he appears within thirty days of receipt of my card, I am fortunate, indeed. But Mr. Sandoval may be summoned by telephone. It is in his home. Mr. Sandoval's wife

107

always answers the phone and I can hear children chattering away as we discuss plumbing emergencies. Evidently the place Mr. Sandoval calls "The Shop" is in the backyard and removed from telephone distractions.

I first met Mr. Sandoval over the necessity for installation of a new hot-water heater. In the store where I found the kind I wanted, the Anglo clerk was doubtful if that heater could be fitted into the space available for it in my long narrow kitchen. He suggested that I consult with Mr. Sandoval. Mr. Sandoval took measurements, went to the store and appeared at my adobe, riding in the delivery truck along with the heater. "It will fit in all cozy," he assured me. In a twinkling it was set up, attached and producing gallons of hot water.

Then the narrow little gas range, which had served me many years, grew very tired of cooking. To my dismay, I could find no new range like it. All the new ranges were much too wide. Again I called Mr. Sandoval. Again he appeared on the delivery truck. Again he measured and remarked, "This will take some doing."

"Even if the oven door will open only part of the way," I conceded, "I can stand to one side and slip a pie or a pan of cookies in sideways."

Mr. Sandoval measured and calculated. "If we can run the vent from the oven up from the room behind your kitchen, it will give us four or five inches more," he suggested.

"But I don't want an old black pipe up along the wall of that room," I protested.

Mr. Sandoval smiled and twinkled. "You don't have to use an old black pipe. Four dollars more and you have a nice silvery one."

I capitulated to a silvery pipe. Mr. Sandoval cut a hole in the kitchen wall and another in the roof of the next room. In a few minutes he called me. He was fairly dancing for joy. "Open your oven door," he exclaimed and laughed until he wept at my amazement when I found that the oven door could be opened full width and that I did not have to sidle a pan of biscuits into it.

"There's nothing like you native workmen," I exulted.

"And nothing like native adobe houses," echoed Mr. Sandoval. "I've put plumbing fixtures in lots of fine new homes. But those houses do not have what these houses have. I don't know what it is, but they have something."

"Something indefinable," I agreed. "The strength of the indigenous and the whimsicality of the handmade!"

"Say," ejaculated Mr. Sandoval, "some of my friends have told me about a book. They want me to read it—about adobe houses and us Spanish Americans. Something about an old adobe wall."

"*No High Adobe?*" I asked.

"That's it," he nodded. "I never have time to get to the library to find it. Have you read it?"

"Yes," I chuckled.

"Any good?"

"*Poco más o menos,* more or less," I laughed.

"I sure want to read it," grieved Mr. Sandoval. "But I can't seem to get to the library what with peoples' pipes always stopping up or spring-ing leaks."

"I happen to have a copy you may borrow," I offered.

As I put the book in his hands, he noticed my name on the cover. "Did you write it?"

At my nod, Mr. Sandoval demanded a piece of wrapping paper to protect the cover. "When I'm not reading it," he added, "it goes into the old iron safe I have out in The Shop."

I know books have found themselves in strange places. But possibly this is the first time a little book, bound in old Spanish pink, has been found in the old iron safe of a Spanish-American plumber—right along with a certified copy of his plumber's license.

GRACE BEFORE DOLLARS

*M*any of the Señoras in Tenorio Flat pass through my yard of a morning on their way to work in Anglo homes. Their passing is as erratic as the flight of birds. Few of them seem to work regularly or on stated days.

A study of Mrs. Apodaca's housework engagements and the reasons for them would drive an economist to despair. Mr. Apodaca has a reasonably well-paid labor job with the gas company which he has held for many years with few deflections to attend to more important personal matters. The older children are in homes of their own. "That Carmencita" makes her own spending money in a great variety of exciting activities. But Mrs. Apodaca from time to time glides through my yard, her head bound with a white flour sack and an apron under her arm.

The only Anglo for whom Mrs. Apodaca has worked somewhat regularly is "Mees" Boggers when she first appeared on the Santa Fe scene and went completely regional in home and attire. Mrs. Apodaca considered "Mees" Boggers the "most quaint person I know." "Mees" Boggers reciprocated with the same opinion of her employee.

But, in the course of years, the charm of reciprocal "quaintness" wore off to some extent and now Mrs. Apodaca removes the dust from "Mees" Boggers' museumlike house only when exciting events take place there, such as the arrival of visitors from "Dee-troy-eet."

There is also the Anglo lady whom I know only by Mrs. Apodaca's description as the "Anglo lady with the *cinco muchachos*—five children—all boys and all redheaded." Mrs. Apodaca works there from time to time because, as she says, "*Pobrecita*, poor little one, she needs me. Those boys—always eating! No more do I get the breakfast dishes washed but they want to eat again and it's bread and butter and glasses of milk to geeve them. No more do I get one corner of the house cleaned and turn away for a few minutes when I find it feeled with toy trains, fire engines, red wagons speeling straw and rabbits, and horned toads running in every direction. How those *muchachos* can get so dirty in one day! Before I leave, I take overalls, shirts, underwear, and socks off those *muchachos* and throw them eento the washing machine—and those *muchachos* eento the bathtub. But I weel go back. Their mother, *pobrecita*, needs me." So affirms Mrs. Apodaca, nobility written all over her countenance.

Sometimes Mrs. Apodaca works quite frankly to earn *dinero*. Usually it is to help some insolvent *primo* or *compadre*. Or she may want to give a friend a purple plush case containing a pink brush and comb, or to welcome a new baby with a blue silk coat and matching bonnet. She shops around to get the lowest price on the desired commodity. Into this she divides her hourly wage, thereby discovering exactly how many hours she needs to work. Work ceases when the calculated hours are completed, even if the employer's household is left in some confusion.

When these *dinero*-earning occasions occur, Mrs. Apodaca works for a lady whom I know only as the "new reech Anglo on the Camino." As arrangements for this employment are made over my telephone, I have learned that there is a secret deal between them—not to upset labor standards in the vicinity—whereby the rich new Anglo pays twenty-five cents an hour more than the customary stipend.

Suddenly Mrs. Apodaca stopped working for the rich new Anglo who called me on the telephone after several days. "What has become of Mrs. Apodaca?" wailed the new Anglo. "I need her very badly. If the work is too hard or I haven't paid her enough, I'll make it right. I'm new in this place. If I've hurt her feelings, please find out what I've said or done."

Wrapped in her oldest shawl, Mrs. Apodaca was enjoying an interval of gloomy histrionics as she played the part of an abused worker in the field of housework. Every time we had a sad little neighborly chat, I inserted skillfully (I hoped) a little questioning in regard to working for the rich new Anglo. "Was the work too hard?"

"No, the work was easy," confessed Mrs. Apodaca, tight of lip and stiff of back.

"Does the new rich Anglo perhaps have too many *muchachos?*"

"No, the new reech Anglo has but two *muchachos,* both grown up and in the army of the U Esse." Both are generals according to Mrs. Apodaca.

The next conversation covered the subject of "devices to save the labor" for which Mrs. Apodaca has a great antipathy. The rich new Anglo, it seemed, manned these devices herself. Further conversation verified the fact that the new rich Anglo paid more than the customary wage and broke no bills in paying it.

In time I was forced to probe more deeply. Had the rich new Anglo referred to Mrs. Apodaca or her friends as Mexicans? New Anglos, whether rich or poor, sometimes fall into this mistake.

No, the rich new Anglo always used the word "Spanish," thereby acknowledging descent from *Los Conquistadores*.

I was at the end of every clue when one day Mrs. Apodaca revealed the cause of her martyr role. Wiping away a few tears, she said, "Not once when I left at night, Señora, deed the new reech Anglo say 'Thank you,' not once, Señora."

I sat thinking how the word *gracias* decorates the speech of Tenorio Flat and turns the mundane to sheer poetry. *Gracias á Diós* for a sunny day, for health, for a fruit-laden apricot tree. *Gracias, gracias* if one mentions that a child is pretty or that a geranium is blooming well.

CARMENCITA HITS
A SUPERSONIC BARRIER

*C*alm, early summer days of smoky tree shadows on red adobe and pearly cloud shadows on somnolent turquoise sky have been shattered this year by "that Carmencita." Her almost military stride has been discarded for the speedier flight of her old battered bicycle. She has zoomed at all hours through my yard, pedaling violently, hairpins catapulting from the loosening blue-black braids once bound neatly about her head.

I gathered from Mrs. Apodaca that no Anglo child of any importance was left alone while its parents attended social functions. "That Carmencita" babysat them all. She sold and took orders for small articles such as self-sharpening scissors and self-threading needles. Twice a day she pedaled at full speed to the U Esse Post Office to see what the tide of contest answering had washed up on the Apodaca shore.

Not to be outdone by her energetic daughter, Mrs. Apodaca took much more day work than is her custom and came dragging home at nightfall with not a single comment on the the beauty of the spring sunset as she passed my window. Papá Apodaca was heard all over the neighborhood, after his day's work with the gas company, mending roofs, building sheds and repairing floors for anyone who would hire him. Many were the complaints from those who found their sleep punctuated by the blows of Papá's hammer at almost midnight hours.

It was not until school-opening time that I learned what this united Apodaca front had been facing. Suddenly Mrs. Apodaca worked no more and Papá's hammer no longer shattered the whispering night. "That Carmencita's" bicycle leaned impotently against an adobe wall with one flat tire and a broken chain.

"Come and see," begged a rested and beaming Mrs. Apodaca. "Come and see what my Carmencita has bought." Then she whispered from the shelter of her black shawl, "Eet ees all paid for. I get day work and help. Papá work nights and help. Now ees all paid for to the last *centavo*."

118

Carmencita was in school, but the all-paid-for wonder stood in all its glory along the white wall of her little room. *"Muchos, muchos libros,"* breathed Mrs. Apodaca in awe-struck tones. Indeed there were many, many books, lined like soldiers in their own bookcase. I could not believe my eyes. It was a complete set of encyclopedia in excellent binding. This was no child's edition. It was of adult stature both physically and mentally.

As I stood quite overwhelmed, in walked Señor and Señora Segura to inspect the wonder. They touched the bindings gently with cautious, work-roughened fingers.

"Everytheeng ees in those books," explained Mrs. Apodaca, "everytheeng een all the world. Now my Carmencita can get best grades een U Esse history and curren' events. And wheen she write a piece for English class, she can copy a good one out of those so fine books. That Carmencita read out of them at home. She even takes a book along to read in school. Ah, what a girl ees my Carmencita."

For weeks thereafter, Mrs. Apodaca wandered idly about town in a state of great felicity, bragging about the all-paid-for books and her wonderful Carmencita. "That Carmencita," exulted Mrs. Apodaca, "know how many miles ees from here to the moon. She know all about that red, red star she call Mars. She know what ees a jet plane and how beeg ees Space. She know what weel cost to ride een space ship and where they go. She know about sometheeng she call the barrier of the supersonic. What that may be, I know not. I expect," whispered Mrs. Apodaca, "that weeth all these beeg books, the teacher at school weel call me some day to say that my Carmencita weel skip a grade een school this year. Maybe two grades! I keep my best shawl ready and my high kid shoes all nice and black so I can go down to school to thank the teacher any *momento*."

Within a few weeks Mrs. Apodaca did ripple past my house like an unfurled banner of delight. The long fringe on her best shawl danced elegantly as her high kid shoes twinkled down the dusty adobe path toward school. She was so elated that she could not speak, but waved both arms in a pantomime of joyous anticipation too deep for words.

What was my astonishment the next morning to behold her in her customary uniform of grief, her oldest green-black shawl bound tightly about her like an armor of despair. Then began those strange peregrinations between *Casita* Apodaca and Cousin Canuto's *placita,* with María

120

Lupita and Mrs. Apodaca endlessly seeing each other home, their black-wrapped heads close together in unhappy consultation.

The day came when Mrs. Apodaca needed a fresh audience and installed herself in the big rocker. Although an early autumn fire chuckled in the little fireplace, she refused to loosen so much as a single fold of her armor of grief.

"The teacher say," she wept, "that Carmencita weel have to go back a grade een school if she act the way she do now. Eet ees all the fault of those so-fine books. She do not study at home nor at school. She just reads those so-fine books. Her square rooting ees sleeping. She weel not study the history of the U Esse. She copy her pieces for English class right out of those so-fine books. Teacher say to steal peoples' words ees worse than to steal their *dinero*. For curren' events Carmencita talk about nothing but the barrier of the supersonic. Not even teacher know what that mean. She theenk neither do Carmencita. Señora, do you know anyone who would like to buy those so-fine books—cheap?"

BURRO TRAILS
OR PAVED ROADS

*P*robably nothing
has ever rocked the ancient city of Santa Fe as has
the need for paved roads to accommodate an ever-
increasing tide of automobiles. Not Indians in
complete control of its Spanish seat of govern-
ment, not the roar of wagon wheels down the
Santa Fe Trail, not the Stars and Bars floating
briefly over its Palace of the Governors, have so
shaken the old town to its adobe foundations.

Whenever our City Council decides that a
much-used street needs modern treatment, all
property owners along boundaries are duly notified and may attend the meeting where plans and
costs to the owners may be openly debated. So
intense became the interest that a radio broadcast
was arranged. Now, from time to time, Santa Fe
sits by its firesides these winter nights to listen

122

with chuckling delight or clucking dismay to conflicting eloquence.

Cousin Canuto attends these meetings with as much regularity and enthusiasm as *los muchachos* give to the movies. Anyone would think that he owned hundreds of acres of rusty-red *tierra* on both sides of all little crooked roads threatened with paving—and its bills. If my lights are on when he returns, he stops by to give me an eyewitness account.

El Camino del Monte Sol, the Street of the Sun Mountain, has long been a "good" address for artists, writers, professional photographers and all persons interested in the finer aspects of the old town. Alas, it had also become almost impassable with ruts like small wells into which car wheels descended with consequent damage to inner mechanisms.

After the Council meeting on the proposed paving of this famous street, Cousin Canuto sank gasping with mingled concern and amazement into the big rocking chair.

"Did you hear it over the *rahdio,* Señora? Did you hear the wife of the famous *profesor?* All she wanted was to preserve what she called the Dirt Road District. 'Even if they do call us crackpots,' she added.

"That famous painting fellow surprised me, Señora. He did not sound *artístico*. He sounded *mecánico*. He said he could not afford to keep up his car, so much damage did those ruts do it. Then he jumped to his feet and roared, 'The day of burros is over.'

"A lady got to her feet and agreed. 'This is not the day of the donkey,' she said. 'As for this street being Old Santa Fe, it isn't. Camino del Monte Sol is only about forty years old and in this town, that is young and green.' The wife of *el profesor* wilted like a lily in the summer sun."

It was after the Council meeting concerned with the paving of the street I call Chamisa Road that Cousin Canuto burst into Spanish-flavored oratory. Chamisa Road is not far from my own adobe. In its lower reaches, it curves its dusty rutted way toward other streets that lead to the Plaza. In its upper reaches, it curves upward toward the hills and has few houses along its way. Here blossoms the orange-shaded chamisa sage in autumn; here straggle the piñón and cedar forests; here *el piñonero* spreads his sky-blue wings in flight and round-eyed rabbits peer anxiously at my intrusion. I could not imagine my favorite walk paved and curbed any more than I could imagine Cousin Canuto in white tie and

124

tails. As I own no property on Chamisa Road, any protest from me would have been strictly out of order.

But Cousin Canuto not only attended the meeting, he let loose a flood of Hispanic eloquence. Three-quarters of the property owners voted against the innovation of paving. "Señora," he asked, "Why did the Mayor of the City call me Guillermo Hennings Bryán after I speak a few words?"

"William Jennings Bryan was a silver-tongued orator not so many years ago," I explained. I was beginning to wonder about the nature of Cousin Canuto's "few words."

"Ah, Señora," sighed Cousin Canuto," I feel so sad for the lady who has much land where the road runs up toward the hills. It will cost her much money to pave along all that land. She was not at the meeting, but her *abogado,* lawyer, pleaded for her, and I could have wept with shame for the way our town was treating a lady who has given us much—land for our museums, a club for our young people, even a shelter for little lost animals.

"Long years ago she built her home on the top of Chamisa Hill. All she asked was peace and quiet with her music, her books, her friends and

125

good works. And how do we repay her, Señora? We talk about breaking into her quiet hilltop retreat with snorting road machinery, clanking cément mixers, the wild confusion of curb building to be followed by *carros* and truckies shrieking by her home all day and most of the night when the work is finished."

Cousin Canuto mopped his eyes with a red bandanna. "Even at that, Señora, that lady was in a better position to face that paving business than were the Spanish people who live in little adobe houses closer to town. To pay for that paving, even on time, they could not do. So," Cousin Canuto hereupon rose to his feet addressing an imaginary audience, "I say, 'The price you ask for paving may be all right, but we cannot pay it. If you go through with it, we will lose our homes.' "

Waving eloquent arms, he continued, " 'It takes three things to make a sale—an article for sale, someone who wants it, and money to pay for it. Now you have the article for sale which is paving. But we don't have the money and besides, we do not want it. I say we DO NOT WANT IT!' At that point, Señora, the Mayor rapped for order and asked if my name is Guillermo Hennings Bryán."

126

Cousin Canuto had almost reached the door, making a grand exit, when I voiced a question that had been perplexing me all through the oratorical recital. "I didn't know you owned any property on Chamisa Road," I questioned. "Perhaps you have a little lot there which some ancestor left you?"

Cousin Canuto straightened himself to full oratorical posture. "No, Señora," he replied calmly. "I do not own one inch of land along any roads they want to pave. As you know, my little house is two miles away from any paving project and in another direction."

CÉMENT OR ADOBE

*W*hen lilacs outlined the confines of the older part of Santa Fe with scrollwork of lavender, when apple blossoms stenciled themselves against brown adobe walls, nest-acquiring became the order of the day. Birds and humans seemed to have a common aim.

"Mees" Emily became involved through two sisters, the Sisters Wintermute of Philadelphia. After spending many vacations in Santa Fe, the sisters were determined to transplant their roots in adobe. Would "dear Emily" look the real-estate situation over and select a likely site or two before they moved themselves and their mahogany furnishings adobe-ward?

Reluctantly "Mees" Emily left her lovely patio where white-winged pigeons skim the sun-filled air. She left her blue and yellow irises that were just coming into bloom. She left her tall pear tree which was wearing a silver crinoline of

blossoms. She left her new book of poetry and became involved with a real-estate lady who was given to the use of the adjective "sweet."

"Mees" Emily was confident that the Sisters Wintermute would want an adobe house much like her own. The only stipulation they had made was that the house should have two bathrooms.

After many days of walking in and out and around adobe houses with the real-estate lady, "Mees" Emily sank into my big rocker. I noticed that she was wearing her Indian moccasins which are usually reserved for the vast rough stretches of the Navajo reservation.

"Adobe houses are at a premium," gasped "Mees" Emily. "They are in the antique class. At last we found one that the real-estate lady assured me was simply sweet: but it had only one bathroom. But it was an honest little house. I wired my friends that they would have to build the second bathroom. They wired back to look at more modern adobes.

"Have you seen these modern adobes? They are not adobes at all—cinder brick, covered with chicken wire and cement, painted more or less the color of adobe. Great fireplaces built in the middle of a wall and not in a corner! They smoke! You should see the walls! Ceiling beams made of planks antiqued-white! But some of them did have a second bathroom. But to get them you had to buy a much larger house. I'm wiring my friends that it's the 'sweet' adobe or nothing."

Within a few days, "Mees" Emily telephoned that the sisters had wired a small token payment to hold the "sweet" adobe. They and their ancestral mahogany were practically en route. She had returned to the peace of her patio, her irises, her shimmering pear tree, and her new book of poetry.

The next day, Cousin Canuto strode into my house in a state of scintillating excitement. "Señora, you must have heard of Ambrosio Ulibarri of the county of Rio Arriba. He is *político* and now has the promise of a fine job at the Capitol if someone gets elected this November. Ambrosio has sold his *ranchito* in the county of Rio Arriba and wants me to look for a house in Santa Fe for him."

"Adobes are scarce," I warned. " 'Mees' Emily has been wearing her moccasins out to find an adobe for her friends who are moving here from Philadelphia."

"Ah," smiled Cousin Canuto, "You and I and Mees Emily like the little adobes. But Ambrosio is high-power *político*. The little house of adobe would not be proper for him. I must find modern house for him."

"That should be easier," I sighed. "Just go to one of the new real-estate tracts, you blocker of paved streets."

That very day, he called me to gloat over a fine new house with two baths which he had found in a newly built tract. It was, I gathered from his enthusiastic description, a California bungalow-type with what seemed to be Swiss-chalet embellishments as to roof line.

131

Almost simultaneously, "Mees" Emily's friends and their ancestral mahogany arrived in town with the *politico,* Ambrosio, his family and a van full of furnishings. "Mees" Emily and her real-estate lady guided the Sisters Wintermute to the "sweet" adobe. Cousin Canuto and his real-estate operator guided the great *politico* and his family to the California bungalow.

Within a few hours, "Mees" Emily and Cousin Canuto sat wringing their hands in my house. The Sisters Wintermute did not like the adobe. They liked it so little they were willing to forfeit their token payment. *Politico* Ambrosio and family did not like the California bungalow any better. My own adobe congealed with misery.

At that moment, in walked Ambrosio guided by one of Cousin Canuto's *muchachos.* Ambrosio was a handsome Spanish American with the manners of a grandee and a gentle voice. He soothed Cousin Canuto's anguish by remarking that the California bungalow was a very good house, but not suitable for a *paisano,* country person, like himself. He calmed "Mees" Emily by inquiring about her flowers.

"Mees" Emily explained that her friends could not get their ancestral mahogany into the "sweet" adobe she had found for them. Suddenly

132

Ambrosio's face lighted with a great thought. "Mees Emily, please call your real-estate lady and show me that little adobe. Canuto call your real-estate operator and ask him to show that fine bungalow to Mees Emily's friends."

Everyone was trying to telephone at once. There were hurried explanations and running exits.

By night it was all settled. The Sisters Wintermute had always wanted to live in a California bungalow—located in Santa Fe, of course. The great *político* had found the proper background for his señora's loom and her big iron cookstove.

I shall keep my eyes on Ambrosio Ulibarri these next ten years. It may be that he will have to move again—perhaps into that many-winged house on a hilltop which New Mexico has built for its governors.

MISS VALERIA'S BANDIT

*O*ne early summer afternoon, I found "Mees" Emily and Ambrosio, the great *politico* of the county of Rio Arriba, rocking with laughter in "Mees" Emily's lily-scented garden. As I approached, I heard Ambrosio say, "There we were that dark night, lost in the wilds of Nabahoo Land, and someone on horseback came galloping closer and closer."

"Sit down," welcomed "Mees" Emily. "Ambrosio has just returned from skippering the Sisters Wintermute in their new car up into the wilds of the Navajo reservation. Now, Ambrosio, tell it all over again. You won't hear a better yarn all summer."

Ambrosio, wiping tears of laughter from his eyes, steadied his voice. "Miss Lucretia, the younger of the Sisters Wintermute, who bought the fine California bungalow, no sooner got the pictures of her ancestors on the walls than she bought a little car. Nothing would do but I must drive those two white-haired ladies to the Land of the Nabahoos where I have never been. You would not believe it, Señora, but those two ladies have piles and piles of Wild West stories, both in books and *periódicos*."

"You see," put in "Mees" Emily, "the situation *político* is at a stalemate now and Ambrosio had to earn some *dinero*."

"I tell them," sighed Ambrosio, "that the old ones of my people always say *los* Nabahoos were a fierce tribe in days gone by. Nabahoos raided our Spanish villages and carried off the fruits of our hard-earned harvests, yes and even our big looms and yes a good weaver or two to teach them how to weave with the wool of the sheep which they had never done before.

"I tell them all this and Miss Valeria say, 'You hear, Lucretia! The land of the Navajos is no place for ladies of our years. Now, now, Lucretia!'

"Miss Valeria has been saying, 'Now, now, Lucretia,' as far back as I can remember," laughed "Mees" Emily. "But it has no effect on Lucretia. Only a few years ago they toured the British Isles by motorcycle. That is, Valeria rode in a sidecar surrounded by luggage and Lucretia manipulated the motorcycle. Another time they took a freighter to the western coast of South America and saw mostly nitrate shipments. Another time they went up the coast of Alaska and visited many fish canneries."

"We got as far as Gallup the first day," continued Ambrosio. "Miss Lucretia rode in front with me and Miss Valeria sat in back and crocheted something most of the way. We had a nice civilized place to stay that night. But the next day we got nowhere fast because Miss Lucretia had to stop to take the picture, to gather rock specimens and to sketch a 'choice bit.' With only crackers and cheese for lunch and with a dark stormy night coming down, we found ourselves out in an endless waste of empty country. It stretched on and on, all fierce red rocks, sheer cliffs, and not a house in sight. At last, far ahead in the fast-falling night, I thought I saw something that looked like a human habitation.

" 'A trading post!' cried Miss Lucretia. 'Maybe the trader will take us in for the night and give us some supper!'

"I drove as fast as I could over a road that was all deep ruts one minute and drifted sand the next. Poor Miss Valeria leaned forward over the back of the front seat to feast her eyes on a house at last. We were all tired, dusty, and very hungry.

"After what seemed endless miles, we stopped in front of the building. It was a trading post! But it was closed tight as a drum. There wasn't a light in it.

"We sat like three deflated balloons. We didn't know where to go from there or what to do next. We just sat.

" 'Someone is coming toward us over there,' whispered Miss Lucretia. 'Someone on horseback. Listen, you can hear the hoofbeats.'

" 'It's a Navajo,' gasped Miss Valeria. 'A bandit!'

" 'Did you bring your revolver?' Miss Lucretia hissed in my ear. I shook my head in great despair.

"At breakneck speed the horseman neared us and pulled up his horse. It was a Nabahoo all right. He wore white pants and a blue velveteen shirt. A red *banda* was around his head, and turquoise and silver jewelry hung around his neck, dangled from his ears, and twinkled on his fingers and his wrists.

"I could feel poor little Miss Valeria's arms shaking as she leaned against the back of the front seat. There was a terrible silence.

137

" 'Good evening, friends,' smiled the Naba-hoo. 'Are you in any trouble? Can I help you?'

" 'We're lost,' confessed Miss Lucretia. 'We need a place to stay the night and something to eat and gallons of hot water.'

" 'Just follow me,' beckoned the Nabahoo. 'A few miles down the road is a place where they are good to people.'

"After several miles of rough roads, the Nabahoo stopped in front of a rambling, poorly lighted building in the midst of dark shrubbery and darker trees.

" 'Now, now, Lucretia,' shuddered Miss Valeria. 'Don't you dare go near that dark house. It's probably a trap.'

" 'It's a mission school,' chuckled the Naba-hoo as he led us to the door. 'The teachers are either at Prayer Meeting or correcting papers in their rooms.'

"In no time at all we were fed, bathed and asleep in great beds whose sheets smelled of desert sunshine. The next morning after break-fast, Miss Lucretia asked one of the teachers, 'Was that a Navaho chieftain who guided us here?'

"The teacher laughed and laughed. 'Chief-tain! That was Joe John Begay. He went to school here for years and years. I taught him to read and write English myself. Sometimes I thought he was pretty dumb. But he's just back from the University of California. He came back with his Master's in education.' "

BIRD WATCHERS, UNITE!

*N*ow that summer is dancing in and out of our high country on sprightly slippers of the wind, Cousin Canuto seems to be a daily visitor in my yard. Sometimes I find him peering into the tall branches of the silver maples or stalking up and down the lilac hedge.

"Ah, Señora," he explained, "I am now a bird watcher. Mees Boggers asked me to put my name on a paper for a club she call 'Bird Watchers, Unite.' I am now a bird watcher. I watch *los piñoneros,* those handsome fellows of the blue, blue wings and the not-so-handsome voices. I watch the big-chested ones with the red vests and others with names I know not. Although she did not explain, I suppose Mees Boggers will invite us all to her *casita* some night soon and we will each tell the names of the birds we have watched. Alas, Señora, I do not know the names of many, but I will learn as I listen to the others. In these days of hurry, it is a happy occupation. I have Mees Boggers to thank that I am now a Bird Watcher United."

I told Cousin Canuto about the migrating grosbeaks, hundreds of them, which sometimes use the silver maple trees as a one-night *posada*, inn. I promised that should they accept my hospitality again, I would dispatch any long-legged *muchacho* I might find in my yard to skim up the footpath beside the water "deetch" to alert Canuto to come at full speed to observe the beguiling birds.

After that, Cousin Canuto enlarged his field of bird-stalking. Whenever I walked to the Plaza, I would see him prowling in the yards of total strangers or scanning the topmost branches of cottonwood trees along the Alameda. I sighed to think that the faithful María Lupita would again be taking over her husband's duties in the little store in addition to caring for a family of nine.

One late afternoon Cousin Canuto spied me and forgot his bird watching long enough to relate that Mees Boggers had called a meeting of "Bird Watchers, Unite" for that very evening in her *casita*. "I have only a few birds I can report," bewailed Cousin Canuto, *"los piñoneros,* robins, bluebirds, woodpeckers, and of course, sparrows and finches. I will probably have the smallest list of anyone there. But it has been a happy time for me. It is resting to my thoughts which are so often disturbed by large affairs like a uranium strike or matters *políticos*. The other bird watchers will have many more birds on their lists. I had counted on the grosbeaks, but unhappily they are delayed in their journey."

The next morning, a perplexed and utterly crestfallen Cousin Canuto dropped into a chair beside me. Although a cold, gusty rain was falling, he sat mopping his heated brow with a red bandanna.

"How was the bird watcher meeting?" I asked. "Did the others add to your list of birds?"

Cousin Canuto peered at me with questioning eyes. "Perhaps because I was the only Spanish person present, Mees Boggers called on me first of all to report what I knew. What I knew were her very words. I mentioned *los piñoneros*, robins, bluebirds, redheaded woodpeckers and, of course, sparrows and finches. There was a great silence, Señora, and some ripples of laughter. Mees Boggers hurried to call on other people.

"One reported that the road from the east into Santa Fe was the only way into town that had

142

any charm and quaintness left, and now they were talking about making it wider. Everyone groaned and said harsh things about the road department. Can a road be a bird, Señora?

"Another bird watcher said that a TV company wanted to build a high tower on the hills very close to the ruins of old Fort Marcy which was built when *los americanos* took over the country. Every bird watcher became very angry and a resolution was passed to outtalk the City Council on the spot at their next meeting. Can a TV tower be a bird, Señora?

"Mees Boggers talked a long time about the neon signs on stores along the plaza and every bird watcher threatened not to buy so much as a spool of thread in those stores. It went on and on. New houses being built that looked like California bungalows or houses from the Swiss Alps! I was asked to go to a bird watchers' meeting, and all I heard about was charm and quaintness and the good old days when everyone got his water out of a blue-covered well and everyone painted the pretty picture or wrote the nice poetry. Has anything gone wrong with my head, Señora?"

I laughed until I wept as I remembered. Some time ago our City Council or Chamber of Commerce had suggested that some more productive occupations must be provided for the people in our old town. Quaintness was not exactly covering the budget. It was predicted in our local paper that every effort would be fought by the "bird watchers." "But," advised the paper, "let the bird watchers move away if they don't like it."

The battle was on! At that, one of Santa Fe's most distinguished writers had replied in the paper with a bugle-toned article headed "Bird Watchers, Unite." Since then, anyone who wants to keep even a few of the delightful old ways or locations here is called a bird watcher, even if he does not know a robin from a grosbeak. Of course the inflammable "Mees" Boggers had collected quickly all the bird watchers she could find for concerted action, even the unsuspecting Cousin Canuto.

Soon he was laughing with me. "Señora," he chuckled, "I think I resign from the 'Bird Watchers, Unite.' My people live here many years and we know that what is new at one time will be quaint later on. But I still will watch *los pajaritos,* the birds. They rest my mind from the affairs *importantes.*"

"Cousin Canuto," I confessed, "I, too, am a watcher of *los pajaritos.* I am also the other kind of bird watcher—from the bottom of my heart."

144

FREE ENTERPRISE

*M*rs. Apodaca suddenly began working with amazing regularity in "Mees" Boggers' museumlike adobe. The reason for this unusual activity was that my neighbor had determined to equip Carmencita with two print dresses featuring the bouffant skirts over stiff petticoats that have practically blocked the narrow sidewalks of Santa Fe and seemingly turned them into a promenade for huge, inverted hollyhocks.

After the first day's work Mrs. Apodaca stopped by at night to report the breathtaking news that "Mees" Boggers planned to sell her adobe and move to some other town in the region. "Mees Boggers say Santa Fe have changed too much. She do not like the lights for the traffic nor the meters for the *automóvil*." Mrs. Apodaca shuddered in excellent mimicry of her employer and exclaimed, "But most of all Mees Boggers ees unhappy about the lights she call 'neon' on branches of beeg stores from far away. They spoil our streets around our old Plaza, she theenk. Lots of nights she go down and seet on bench in Plaza and weep because of those ugly glaring lights."

Within a few days I learned that "Mees" Boggers had been to Taos in search of untainted locale for another museumlike adobe and had returned in the depths of despair. Taos, it seemed, in spite of its blue, blue atmosphere, and its many artists, also had parking meters around its plaza and other evidences of the mechanical age.

In time she visited Mora, Las Vegas, and even the Spanish villages of Truchas and Trampas, only to find deepfreeze compartments in village stores and trucks and cars roaring through village streets. With great joy, Mrs. Apodaca reported that "Mees" Boggers had relinquished the thought of abandoning the field of battle. She had decided to stand her ground and fight it out on the home front. "She theenk," confided Mrs. Apodaca, "eet ees too late to fight the lights of the traffic and the meters for the *automóvil*. But she weel fight to a feenish the bright lights on some of the stores around our Plaza at night."

146

For a few days I was left in ignorance of what "Mees" Boggers' strategy in the "fight to a feenish" against the offensive lights along our Plaza might be. Mrs. Apodaca was searching methodically and slowly the old established stores where she had always done her buying. With frustrated headshaking and much sighing she reported that dresses such as she wanted for Carmencita were *muy, muy caras*—very expensive. She would not buy at such a price if she had to wait until snowfall.

But at last "Mees" Boggers' strategy in the "fight to a feenish" took her whole attention. Mrs. Apodaca appeared with a long paper which stated that the undersigned agreed not to buy so much as a spool of thread in the offending stores until they removed the glaring neon lights. Mrs. Apodaca's name graced the first line of a paper she was to take to all her Spanish friends for their signatures. "Mees" Boggers had her paper, I learned, headed by the name of "Mees" Emily. Evidently the stategy was to boycott all of the neon-lighted stores around the Plaza.

After that, a dusty-of-shoe and bedraggled Mrs. Apodaca plodded through my yard, bound for Spanish signatures. But Spanish Americans did not seem to be boycott-minded. They were not signing in any great numbers. "Mees" Boggers was meeting with greater success. She had several hundred names, it was reported.

It was "Mees" Emily who first deserted the ranks. Mrs. Apodaca, positively shaking with emotion, burst into my adobe one night to whisper that "Mees" Emily had been seen emerging from the most blatant of the boycotted stores with an immense package in her arms.

As it turned out, her motives for defection were aesthetic rather than economic as suspected. "Mees" Emily makes her own beautiful regional dresses. Some of the most elaborate are made of the cheapest and most sleazy unbleached muslin. She dyes the muslin unbelievable colors which she concocts much as a lady of the Victorian age fashioned a potpourri of flower petals. The cheap sleazy material takes the dye far better than the closely woven, more expensive muslin.

"Mees Emily was very nize," approved Mrs. Apodaca. "She go right over to tale Mees Boggers what she have deed and why. I was working for Mees Boggers and she say, 'What was I to do, Eudora?'"

"I know," I interrupted, "She came down to tell me. 'There I was,' she groaned, 'confronted with a luncheon, an art exhibit and a reception for a famous archaeologist. I had to have some new clothes.' ''

"Sí," nodded Mrs. Apodaca, breathless to resume her place as raconteur of exciting drama. "She go to all the old stores where she always buy and now cannot find one yard of that cheap cloth she want.

"Why a reech lady like Mees Emily want to buy such cheap cloth I know not," puzzled Mrs. Apodaca. "And she cannot wait for the stores to send away for eet weeth all those fine parties coming so queek."

Mrs. Apodaca rocked and smiled to keep me waiting for the crises I knew as well as she.

At last she straightened in her chair, shuddered and declaimed, "Mees Emily walk right eento one of those stores she promised never to go een. And got lots of other peoples never to go een! That store have two beeg bolts of that cheap cloth she want to make party dresses. She buy both bolts!

"That's why she take her name off Mees Boggers' leest. She ees honest lady even eef she do buy cheap cloth wheen she could buy satin and velvet. ¡Verdád!''

Mrs. Apodaca sighed. "When other Anglo ladies on the leest heard that Mees Emily had taken her name off, they called up and took their names off, too. Mees Boggers was very sad."

A short time after this, Mrs. Apodaca came winging over to see me. In either outstretched hand was a dress with bouffant skirt, stiff lace-trimmed petticoat, and puff-sleeved blouse for Carmencita. One was yellow with yellow embroidery on the white blouse. The other was dull blue with a blouse of lighter tone. "Where did you find them?" I exclaimed. "They are lovely."

"I hunt in every store in town, Señora, and find them at last in store weeth the light of the neon. I buy. Like Mees Emily I go right up and tale Mees Boggers and take my name off leest. After I do that, all the other Spanish ladies take their names off, too. There ees not one left. Mees Boggers ees very sad again."

"Why did you buy in that boycotted store?" I asked out of sheer curiosity. Then I settled back in my chair, thinking my neighbor would take at least a quarter of an hour explaining. She did nothing of the kind. Eyes shining, she explained her position in just three words. "They were cheaper," she said, amazement at my stupidity mingling with the lilt in her voice.

DEFERRED DESIGN

*G*randmother Anaya, Abuela Anaya, lives alone in a little crooked-walled adobe house as diminuitive as herself. Swathed in enfolding black shawl and trailing long black skirts, she looks more like a wisp of black cloud than a person skimming the rutted red paths of Tenorio Flat.

Most of the space in Abuela Anaya's house is taken up by an enormous loom made long, long ago. With poorly concealed pride she always manages to bring into the conversation the regal announcement that she is descended from one of the most famous of weaving families in the orchard-sweet valley of Chimayó where, even to this day, almost every adobe home still echoes to the song of the loom.

Abuela Anaya, unlike many weavers of today, dyes most of her yarn herself, with skillfully prepared vegetable coloring contrived from bark, shrubs and flowers. She follows no pattern of design. Her designs come to her, she says, right out of her *corazón*, her heart. With her little crooked home and the earnings from her weaving, she has always managed a proud independence.

From time to time, the song of the loom ceases in the little crooked house and it echoes with the laughter and excited chatter in Spanish of some of Abuela's many grandchildren. Because of these frequent visitations of enraptured grandchildren, I thought nothing of evidence of their presence. Who would not want to visit a tiny grandmother in a tiny storybook house? But a few snowy winters ago this evidence lingered week after week in the form of daily baby washings freezing stiff on the clothesline behind the little crooked house.

Later I discovered Abuela in snow above her shoe tops, struggling with frozen baby clothes as stiff as boards. Tossing Spanish decorum to the wintry winds, I blurted out, "Your grandchildren are making a long visit this time."

"They are not visiting me," said the shivering little woman, raising her gentle voice above the shrieking wind. "They lose their mamacita. So I take them."

152

"How many?" I demanded in consternation.

"Three," answered Abuela calmly.

"How old?" I gasped.

"The baby, Salvador, has but three months; and the leetle girls, Dolores and Diolinda, have two and three years."

"Surely someone else could take them from among all your married children," I protested.

"All have the beeg beeg families. Some say they take one. Some say they take another. Better these babies grow up together. So I take."

"How long do you expect to keep them?"

"So long they need," answered Abuela in a matter-of-fact voice.

"But your weaving! No one can weave like you, Abuela!"

"I weave no more. The babies' papá, poor boy, has leetle work. He gives us what he can. I make the leetle clothes for them by hand at night. I have no *máquina* to do the sewing. Some I make from old flour sacks. But I take leetle steetches and try to make them pretty."

"It is too, too hard for you," I protested, looking at the frail little grandmother.

Abuela Anaya straightened up in the wintry wind. I shall never forget the light in her eyes nor the proud smile on her face. "It is hard," she agreed reasonably. Then she gave me a compassionate smile. "They are my sohn's children," she said with finality.

For two years and eight months that tiny grandmother pitted herself against frozen washings, summer heat and the irregular contributions of relatives. Then one golden October day when aspen gold was sifting down the mountainsides, I saw her sitting on a low adobe wall with her grandchildren around her. Salvador, the baby, had now almost three years. Dolores and Diolinda would soon be schoolgirls. Their hair fell in lustrous blue-black waves about their shoulders. Their big eyes sparkled. Their ruddy cheeks glowed with much scrubbing. Even in their poor little garments, they seemed the most beautiful children I had ever seen in this land of beautiful children. Their grandmother caught my look of admiration. "Pretty," she acknowledged modestly.

Then she sighed. "Tomorrow they leave me. Their papá has found a new wife who wants the children. She is a good girl, the new mamacita. She comes from my own old village of Chimayó. My sohn has now steady job with Gas Company in Santa Fe. They have rented a house on Agua Fría Street. So *los niños* will come often to see me when their papá and mamacita want to go to a dance or make fiesta."

"You will be lost without those children," I grieved, completely forgetting my lamentations when they first appeared on the scene of the little crooked house. "Whatever will you do without them after all these years?"

Abuela Anaya smiled with girlish anticipation. "Tomorrow I start weaving. Even now I have an order for a beeg blanket from a reech Anglo."

"But haven't you forgotten how to weave? It's been a long time since you have had quiet to dream up a beautiful design."

The tiny weaver laughed at such heresy. "Do I forget how to walk or how to breathe?" Then she drew a corner of her shawl over her mouth to indicate how confidential she considered her next statement. "All the days and nights that I have *los niños* with me, the *corazón* fills with pretty patterns. I theenk when I do washing. I theenk when I cook food. I theenk when I make leetle steetches at night in flour-sack dresses. It will be a fine blanket I weave for reech Anglo. And more and more and more! All different! All out of the full, full *corazón!*"

155

MAGIC CARPETS

*T*he story
and the drama of a modern-day adventure in education has been taking place, appropriately enough, not far from the old "Four Corners," the only place in the nation where four states meet—Colorado, Utah, Arizona, and New Mexico. It is a breathtaking land of sheer red cliffs, strangely sculptured rocks, and interminable stretches of color-daubed desert wastes shadowed by the "points of sacred mountains."

Anything could happen here and has been happening through the centuries. It is a land of dim, prehistoric Indian trails and hidden ruins, of cattle raiders and the tattoo of galloping hoofs, of crawling wagon wheels and the baa-ing of countless Navajo sheep. Recently it has become the land of gigantic pipe lines for natural gas, of new-found oil spattering the ruddy earth and of the talkative geiger counter.

The drama started when six public schools of McKinley County enrolled hundreds of little Navajos, many of whom had never been in school and who spoke no English. Navajo children were mixed in with Anglo children and with children from Spanish-speaking homes. Many of the Anglo children and those from Spanish-speaking homes had attended the same schools. It was the great influx of Navajo children which produced the laughter and the tears, the high endeavor, and the portent of things to come for this drama of education in this ancient highly-colored setting.

Just catching the big orange bus along the highway whisked many a Navajo child from a way of living that was almost medieval. Like some kind of magic carpet, it tossed boys like Sam Chee Jo from the centuries-old security of family and clan, from sheepherding and going for the weekly barrel of water, into the midst of shining lava- tories, endless water, soap, and towels made of paper. He ate strange food for his noonday lunch and ate it with utensils he might never have used before. Even the smallest of schoolrooms looked enormous compared to his wattled hogan, or wooden shanty.

The woman who owned the room with the little chairs and desks was called Teacher. She did not look like his mother at all. Her skirt had hardly any calico in it. She wore very little turquoise and silver jewelry. She must be very poor. His mother had heaped-up handfuls of it—sometimes at home and sometimes on the hard-goods-pole at the trading post. Almost every winter she had to pawn it for flour and canned milk.

It wasn't so bad getting up and walking two or three miles over the hills to catch the bus part of the year. But when winter came, the sun himself didn't get up until late. The school had a thing called a clock, but not his hogan! Busses and teachers paid no attention to the sun. The clock told them when to do everything—when to eat, when to go outdoors, when to go home. It must be Teacher's god of the sky!

Always it was wash, wash hands and face and wear clean, clean pants and shirt. If you haul your water, one barrel a week by horse and wagon from a well four miles across the desert, there is not much left for washing pants and shirt. One night his mother did wash his pants and shirt and it rained and they did not get dry. He had one other pair of pants, but they were torn in all the wrong places. He had to stay home until his good pants

got dry. He could not go to school and Teacher did not like.

But Sam Chee Jo always got to school even when snow lay over the old red-earthed Indian country. It spread over the high red cliffs that stand like man-made battlements and turrets with fantastic sculptured gargoyles against the skyline. Sometimes the wind picked up the snow and blew it in silver pennants and streamers from the topmost pinnacles.

Sam Chee Jo's family did not have a clock, but they had an old battery-run radio that gave them the time. When Sam Chee Jo heard it, he struggled out of his blankets on the earth-packed floor of the hogan. His father went to the door and looked out on the arctic scene. "Go back to bed," he yawned. "The snow will be hip-deep for you along the steep trail to the highway. You can't get to school today."

Sam Chee Jo began to howl like a lone coyote on a snowy, treeless hilltop. He howled and would not eat his breakfast of fried bread nor drink his hot coffee. He put on his coat and heavy shoes, only stopping once in awhile to howl longer and louder. His father put on his sheepskin coat and a big black hat. "Our ears will suffer all day with his howling," he grunted. "I'll get him on the bus if I have to carry him in my arms. It will be worth it to have peace."

So it was that a strange sight appeared along the snow-blotted trail that led between the snow-bannered monstrous battlements. Down the steep hillside where cedar trees sagged with the weight of accumulated whiteness, along the glassy-pink arroyo and up another hillside crept a Navajo man who had never seen the inside of a school. Sometimes he dragged his little boy by main force. When the going was too bad, he carried him in his arms like a baby. Sam Chee Jo smiled under the flakes that matted his eyelashes and tangled his eyebrows.

At last they reached the highway. Sam Chee Jo climbed onto his magic carpet and disappeared in wind-driven snow. His father struggled back down the hill, across the frozen arroyo and up the next hill between the gargoyled battlements. In the afternoon he would repeat the trip. It might go on for days.

"Why," demanded his wife, "does that boy have to go to school when the trail to the bus is buried under snow to his waist?" She stirred the cooking mutton. Fear was on her face. At last she broke the fearful silence. "Maybe he is afraid. Maybe they beat them if they stay away from school."

The Navajo man put down the cup from which he had been gulping hot strong coffee. Wonder was on his face and in his voice. "He is not afraid. I ask him. They do not beat anyone. Sam Chee Jo likes the Learning Paper." He had used the old Navajo words for education.

MYSTERIES
OF "LEARNING PAPER"

*O*f all the people connected with this adventure in education, Navajo mothers probably had the widest and deepest abyss to span. For most of them it stretched from far-flung pastoral living to the clanging uproar of modern America.

Suppose a Navajo mother visited her childrens' school one day and found Teacher busy with a class. Teacher waved a welcoming hand and pointed to an empty chair. The Navajo mother seated herself comfortably on the floor, spreading her long, full skirts about her. She stared at the group of children Teacher had gathered together. Each child held a small hand mirror in front of his face and painstakingly fixed small lips and tongue to form the English "th" sound instead of the Navajo "d." Over and over the children practiced these sounds looking into their hand mirrors.

When Teacher looked up again, the Navajo mother had disappeared. But others followed her. If children were practicing looking-glass sounds, Navajo mothers sank to the floor and watched proceedings wide of eye, but impassive of face.

But when Navajo mothers met at trading post or at a "Sing," one of them must have said, "What do our children with looking glasses in school? Have you seen them? I ask my girl and she makes hissing noises like a little snake."

Another Navajo mother would laugh and say, "I, too, saw the looking-glass class. I think they show our children how to put the white powder on the face and how to paint the lips red the way the Anglo and Spanish women do." But another Navajo mother said, "No, it could not be that. Boys were in the looking-glass class. I saw them with my own eyes. Not even Anglo boys use the white powder on the face nor the red paint on the lips." It remained a mystery.

Or a Navajo mother might take folded papers from the recesses of voluminous skirts. "They keep coming in the hands of the children —these papers with pictures. Look at this one with men of the tall hats and strange clothes and

Indians with bow and arrows and big green trees and a boat with wings on much water."

"That," said the daughter of her brother who had been away to Indian boarding school, "is a kind of Anglo Creation Myth. As we Navajos moved from Blue World to Yellow World, so did the Anglos move. They came from a little land with the sea all around it. They came on a boat with wings. After long time, they see land and go on it and meet Indians with bow and arrows. The Anglos cut down trees and build house to live in and house for their ceremonial and house to learn paper for their children. After first harvest, they have big feast and ask Indians to come and eat and keep the Day of Giving Thanks."

"And this one," persisted the Navajo mother, "of the fat Anglo in the red clothes and long white beard! Is he a *santo* as the Spanish have in their churches? He looks too fat to be a *santo*. *Santos* do not eat much. They are very thin."

Navajo mothers did not let their children down even when bean necklaces and paper-plate potholders followed the art work. They hung the bean necklaces around their necks along with their priceless silver and turquoise. They nailed the potholders to a convenient board in the hogan wall as an ornament. The mothers exclaimed and smiled as they were expected to do. But they wondered, "Was it for this that we gave up the help of our children in herding the sheep, in going for water, in bringing in wood, in taking care of the baby? Was it for this that someone had to walk with the children twice a day over the hills to take them to and bring them from the big orange bus?" It was a mystery.

Then there was something called "Peetie-A." Navajo parents were urged to go along with Spanish and Anglo parents. You could even bring the babies and no one said anything if they cried when people talked. They talked in Spanish and English and Navajo.

Out of all this talking, mysteriously came lots of work like schoolyard cleaning and tree planting and earning money for the little pills that were supposed to keep the children as frisky as lambs in spring. There were long, long talks and laughing and singing mixed in with cups of hot coffee and cakes with a hole in the center. "Peetie-A" was evidently an Anglo clan.

When the children gave plays or sang or showed their work in school, Navajo mothers filled the rooms. They looked at all the different kinds of children and decided that their own looked just as happy and sang as hard and acted just as nice as the others. One thing they worried about. Would their children look just as happy when they grew up? Or would they look like many of the grown-up Anglos? Would they be watching that time-snipper on their wrists? Would they have to hurry, hurry to earn more money to buy more things? That was another mystery. Grandmother Navajo felt the mystery, too. On the way home in the pickup, she said, "Will our children keep on walking the Beautiful Way?"

After several years of this big adventure in "Learning Paper," it begins to look as if it had not been bought at the price of losing cultural individuality. Neither has the price been the separation of the generations. A Navajo schoolboy was asked what he was going to do on his vacation. He was a run-of-the-mill Navajo boy with black hair, dark eyes and high cheekbones. He played baseball, went to the movies, read the comics, speculated on spacemen and thought a hot dog and bottle of pop made a banquet.

"The first thing I've got to do on my vacation," he answered, "is to take my BB gun and go up in the hills and shoot a lot of bluebirds."

The teacher had a moment of despair. For years they had been teaching the children to be kind to furred and feathered friends. They had fed the birds at school on wintry window sills. They had adopted a robin with an injured leg and arranged quarters and food for a little lost lamb. Why this slaughter of beautiful birds which no one would eat?

Then the teacher remembered. This young Navajo was the grandson of a medicine man. Bluebird feathers were an essential ingredient of certain ceremonials of his people. For all the spacemen and baseball and movies, this young Navajo was running true to his cultural pattern.

A middle-aged Navajo found his way into the Gallup public library. He was a run-of-the-mill Navajo in working man's clothes and a big black hat. He stood for a moment looking at the beautiful hand-carved chairs and tables, at the specimens of Indian pottery and at the pictures by Indian artists on the walls. There were rows and rows of shelves filled with books all around him. He eyed them with evident relief. He had found the right place.

He went to the librarian and said in his limited English that he wanted a book that held English words—all of them.

The librarian grasped his meaning in a moment. "Oh, a dictionary," she said. "Right over here," and led him to a massive Webster's on its metal stand.

"Too big," the Navajo shook his head. "Want book to carry around."

The librarian brought a collegiate edition from the shelf and put it in his hands.

"Good, good," approved the Navajo and pulled out his purse. "How much," he asked.

The librarian explained that she did not sell books. People took them home to read. Did he want a card so he could take the dictionary home? It would cost him nothing.

"No, no," exclaimed the Navajo. "Want to buy."

"You will have to go to a bookstore," explained the librarian, and told him where to find one nearby.

As the Navajo was leaving he said, "Want book for present for my boy. He go to high school next year."

UNKNOWN TO MAN

*J*n hot but stealthy pursuit of a dream, Simón Casados hid his light pickup truck behind a clump of parched cedar and piñón trees. Here the New Mexican sheep trail frayed out in a welter of rocks. So far, Indian Pete's map drawn on a scrap of dirty paper was all right. It had better be! Simón had paid out ten dollars in tired-looking bills to the Indian for that map. Through the years he had paid out a lot of money for such maps. Simón for all his graying hair, his girth and full-moon face was hag-ridden by a dream.

Now there was nothing for it but to climb over two pathless ridges. The top of one was marked by an outcropping of pink sandstone shaped like an elephant. The sides of the other, Indian Pete had said, were honeycombed with the cliff dwellings of "those who are gone."

Simón loosened the silver concha belt that bound his middle like a barrel hoop. Steaming and puffing, he finally reached the pink elephant. From there he could see the Las Vegas highway from which he had turned onto the sheep trail. Running the Feed and Fuel store at Cottonwood Corners had its points, Simón thought. He could get away. Juan Diego couldn't get away. He was a county sheriff. Ever since they were *muchachos* they had been hunting for the same thing—a trout pool unknown to man. Juan Diego had bought plenty of maps himself and gone off on secret expeditions of his own. Neither one of them had ever found that pool even in the vast uncharted country of northern New Mexico where streams have a way of disappearing and emerging in unexpected places.

Simón chuckled. Juan Diego wouldn't be out looking for trout pools today. A *loco* had escaped from the asylum in Vegas. The *rahdio* had said he was a dangerous *loco*. Juan Diego would be out hunting him.

Blundering down the side of the last range, Simón thought he saw a thread of green in the canyon below. That was where he got to going too fast and rolled the last hundred feet. When he stood up, he couldn't believe his eyes. Indian

170

Pete's map hadn't been like all the others. He had practically rolled into his dream. He had found it first. Juan Diego couldn't laugh this off.

That pool was just as he had seen it in forty years of dreaming. Green water like liquid jade flowed deep between polished boulders. On one side was the pink labyrinth of rocks through which he had come. On the other, snow-topped peaks reached for the blue sky. Not a fisherman in sight, muddying up the water and hanging himself to the alders with his own tackle!

Simón's hands shook so he could hardly get his mail-order-house rod together. He could hardly get his flies off the leather band around the crown of his big black hat. His first cast went wild, but it didn't matter. At his next, there was a rush in the jade-green water. The rod bent and the reel sang its spine-tickling song. Simón almost shook to pieces as he guided that first trout into the landing net. Sixteen inches long it was, firm and fat and silver-spotted.

Another and another Simón played and slipped into the old creel lined with alder leaves. Then a terrible sight met his eyes. Upstream a little way, a wisp of smoke was blowing from behind a boulder. Someone else was here! Indian Pete had double-crossed him and sold the same map to another fisherman. Juan Diego likely! Juan Diego had run out on his high calling of sheriff and was here to laugh at him! *"Hallo, hallo,"* Simón yelled. But there was no answer.

Simón lumbered like a rhinoceros upstream. Behind the great boulder a sickly fire was smoldering. Beside the fire sat the strangest creature he had ever seen. He was an old, thin Anglo with a pale, cadaverous chin sunk in the collar of a long, grey ulster. No fisherman, Simón decided. Not a scrap of tackle in sight! Only a dirty flour sack bulging with something beside the fire!

"Fishin'?" asked Simón just to be saying something.

"No," muttered the creature and kept on writing on scraps of paper he pulled from the yawning pockets of his ulster.

"Prospectin'," surmised Simón, looking at the flour sack.

"No," mumbled the creature and irritably scratched out the last words he had written.

"How'd you get here?" marveled Simón.

"Walked," muttered the creature and waved a vague hand in the direction of the Vegas highway behind the ridges. He kept on writing.

Simón gave it up, thankful that the strange creature was not another fisherman. Back he went to his dream pool and his fishing. He took it easier now, savoring every cast as the saints savor paradise.

Cottonwood fluff clouds began to roll up behind the mountains. Simón cast a weather-wise eye in their direction. At this altitude it might snow before night. Better get out while he could. Then he remembered the old Anglo by the puny fire. He would freeze before morning.

Back he lumbered upstream. "If you think you can hike over the ridges, I'll give you a lift in my truck to a bus so you can go wherever you came from."

Surprisingly the creature stood up on his long heron legs. Simón picked up the flour sack. Heavy as lead it was. The long heron legs could travel, Simón admitted, as he groaned and puffed up the grade behind him. When they got to the Feedena Pigena truck, the creature climbed nimbly in and sank his cadaverous jaw back in the folds of his ancient ulster. Not a word would he say to all of Simón's priming. He seemed sunk in his own consuming thoughts.

It got on Simón's nerves. When a sickly moon came out from behind the clouds and cast a weird light on flat mesa tops and grotesque buttes, Simón's slow brain came alive. Now he

173

knew what he had on the seat beside him. The *loco,* of course! The one that had escaped from that place in Vegas! The one Juan Diego was supposed to take dead or alive!

Simón rocked with laughter. Then he got to thinking. *Locos* were said to have a strength far beyond their age and size. Just suppose—from then on he kept one eye on the road and the other on his companion. When the creature changed his position, Simón felt himself sweating right through the leather band on his battered old hat. It didn't help any when a forlorn coyote started yelping like a lost soul over on a ghostly-green mesa top.

Never had the sparse lights of Cottonwood Corners looked so good. Simón drove straight for the sheriff's shack and yelled for Juan Diego to come out. Then he produced his creel and showed his trout. "I found it," he gloated, "the pool unknown to man."

Juan Diego's black eyebrows went up to his hairline. He couldn't think of a word to say. As an afterthought, Simón produced the creature from the seat of the truck. "Here's the *loco,*" Simón whispered as a crowning insult. "You've probably been wearin' your heels lopsided all day huntin' for him. Get him back you know where!"

Then he jumped in the truck and rattled off down the road. It wasn't until he had stuffed himself with fried trout that he remembered that the creature's old flour sack was still in the truck No matter, he decided, likely as not it was filled with rocks the way it hefted. Then he snorted, thinking of how he had beaten Juan Diego to the pool unknown to man. After all these years! And Juan Diego as sheriff met all kinds of people—forest rangers, dude ranchers and even stray politicians.

Then came a hideous pounding on the door. Had the *loco* escaped from Juan Diego? In stalked the sheriff. He was looking his most ferocious best—cowboy boots, star on his black shirt and eyebrows dead level now. "I've a mind to arrest you," he drawled. "What do ya mean, runnin' off with Professor Terwilliger's Indian relics and the first ten chapters of his new book?"

LOWER COLONIAS

𝓕aced with completing an exacting piece of work as quickly as possible a few summers ago, I became a voluntary prisoner in the Little Adobe House. I saw no one, answered no telephone calls, went nowhere between the hours of nine and five, sometimes working far into the night. "Mees" Emily telephoned from time to time. She always asked unhappily, "Are you still in jail?" When the job was finished, she was the first person I notified.

"That calls for a celebration," she fairly sang. "I'll pick you up within an hour. We'll drive to some lovely part of the country and top it off with a good chile-hot New Mexican dinner at Mr. Salazar's place when we get home. I know you've been eating nothing but sandwiches and canned soup for weeks."

"Mees" Emily knows all the little dirt roads —though somewhat vaguely—in this part of the country. The one she chose led out into the Glorieta-Pecos region where the *tierra* is much redder than it is around Santa Fe and is speckled with elfin forests of piñón and cedar. The roadside looked almost landscaped with carpets of lavender desert verbena and earth-hugging tiny yellow daisies from which swayed tall scarlet penstemon and milkweed spilling silver threads.

When we reached the adobe village of Pecos, I thought that "Mees" Emily would turn up Pecos Canyon where a sibilant stream gossips between decorous pine-clad mountains. The joy of "dirt-roading" with "Mees" Emily is that one never knows where one will eventually find oneself.

True to form, she ignored the beguiling Pecos Canyon road and turned confidently into what seemed little better than a rutted trail. "There's an old adobe village up here a few miles," she chuckled. "I've been wanting you to see it. It's called Lower Colonias. There's an Upper Colonias too, farther back in the mountains, but we haven't time for that this afternoon. The road there is even worse than this one. But I do think old adobe villages should be approached by atrocious roads like this one, not by paved highways."

"Lower Colonias, Lower Colonias," I kept savoring the words, "typical of this bilingual region with part of the name English and part Spanish. 'Lower Colonies' wouldn't be half so melodious."

In spite of sinking into rust-red ruts and dodging rust-red outcroppings of rock in the road, we soon entered the village. Adobe houses spread over a large area—some on sun-polished hilltops, some clinging to the edges of deep arroyos, some in green farmlands along a bend in the river. It took nearly all afternoon to explore the length and breadth of that beguiling village. Little adobe houses, the same color as the good *tierra* from which they sprang, seemed scattered about by some giant salt cellar over the landscape.

Big-eyed children watched our progress. Adults stood in thick-walled doorways and smiled and nodded. Men in farm wagons waved and dodged us expertly along the narrow roads. Spanish flowed up, down and around us. Most of the houses were small, thick-walled adobes with geraniums blooming in old lard cans in deep-set windows. Orange daylilies, lavender and pink asters, and tall hollyhocks bloomed around the old buildings. Then we came to one huge building of almost *hacienda* proportions. There must

178

have been a dozen rooms raying off in wings built at right angles to the main structure All had *portáls* and partially enclosed patios whose lilac bushes must have filled the house with perfume for countless springs.

"Mees" Emily stopped and contemplated the old many-winged house. "Someone lives there," she muttered, pointing to open doors and windows. "How I'd like to come here and board with those people for a month. That old house is full of stories and what a place to get away from it all."

I think "Mees" Emily was secretly disappointed that I did not go immediately into that ancient house and take up a month's residence sans luggage. Reluctantly she turned the car down another rutted road toward the river and soon realized that at last she was on familiar ground. "There used to be a road on the other side of the river under those great white-barked cottonwood trees. We used to picnic there years ago. Someone has bought the land and fenced it in and built some little cabins. They must be for rent. What a place to get away from it all! Let's go talk to that man."

"Mees" Emily is always finding places for me "to get away from it all"—especially month-long incarcerations, be they ever so voluntary. But I was looking at the thick-walled little houses scattered like children's building blocks over the rusty hills above us. "Lower Colonias, Lower Colonias," I repeated the lovely syllables. "What a perfect name for such a place!"

A tall, pleasant man with a Texas drawl greeted us and proudly showed the cabins under the great cottonwood trees. But my thoughts were still firmly twined about the red adobe houses on the red hills back of us. "What a perfect village that is up there," I exclaimed, "and Lower Colonias just suits it for a name."

The *Tejano* glanced upward toward the hills and grinned. "Then it was you two I saw bumping all over the village this afternoon. But, lady, that village isn't Lower Colonias. Lower Colonias is ten miles away in another direction over worse roads. That village up there is called East Pecos." There could be no mistaking the matter-of-fact certainty in his tone. He knew what he was talking about.

Silently and by paved highway, not by dirt road, we reached Mr. Salazar's place. It was not until we had consumed a great platterful of chile-fragrant red beans and cheese-blanketed *enchiladas* with countless crisply bouffant *sopaipillas*

180

that "Mees" Emily regained her composure. "I suppose," she remarked philosophically, "that every human heart cherishes a Lower Colonias which other people call an East Pecos."

A BOOM
COULD BOOMERANG

*D*uring the greatest snowfall
that New Mexico has seen for many a long year,
I became vaguely aware that the people of
Tenorio Flat were glancing in my windows with
unusual interest. One night, almost at dusk, when
I was picking my way through the drifts of the
Flat, I found Cousin Canuto and Carmencita
measuring with a wooden yardstick the distance
between the end of my long yard and that of the
Apodacas. Then Grandpa Segura fairly snatched
the yardstick from Carmencita's hand and started
to measure his tiny lot which separates the Segura's crooked adobe from my own.

If I had not been so engrossed with that prodigious snowfall, I might have realized sooner or
later that I had become an object of wonder to
my Spanish neighbors. After such a storm, ruddy
thick-walled little adobe houses, part and parcel

182

of this sunny arid land, simply entrance me. From prim white neckerchiefs of snow, draped across flat roof edges, to startled deep-set windows, they all have the air of exclaiming, "This couldn't happen to me!" In a few days I was to repeat that exclamation for myself.

Behind those exclamatory windows, the eyes of Tenorio Flat were watching me with undisguised fascination. Sometimes I noticed a small brown hand beckoning to others in the room. Lips formed the words, *"Mira, mira*—look, look, there she goes!"

The explanation came one bitter night, when the corner fireplace was red of face from much singing. In walked Mrs. Apodaca wrapped like a mummy in her black shawl, Cousin Canuto with eyebrows lifted and Carmencita bursting with importance. She fidgeted while the amenities were exchanged and the weather thoroughly analyzed. At last, Cousin Canuto led off with a question. "Señora, if I may make so bold, has anyone tried to buy your *casitas* and big lot?"

"No," I answered in some perplexity, "of course not. They are not for sale."

Cousin Canuto sighed with disappointment. But Carmencita rushed to his aid while Mrs. Apodaca sat tying knots in the corner of her black shawl. "Didn't that man from Texas, who was walking all over your lot just before the snow, try to buy the place? He told Grandpa Segura he wanted to buy it."

"*El Tejano rico* een beeg Cadillac," prodded Mrs. Apodaca.

"There was a man from Texas around just before the snow," I remembered. "I think he was taking pictures as so many people do. He did not ask to come into the house."

"He wouldn't," hissed Cousin Canuto. "That man from Texas was after bigger game than little adobe houses."

Then the amusing episode came clearly to memory. "One day he drove the Cadillac up the driveway and I went out to see what he wanted," I recalled. "He was a very friendly man and his wife and daughters were as pretty as pictures. 'I'd like to buy this place,' he drawled. 'It will make a nice summer home for my family. It gets hot down where we live. No use to look at the houses inside. I'll have to remodel them anyway. I'll fix this one up for my wife and me and the house in front for my married daughter. The little one on the back of the lot under the silver maple trees will make a nice playhouse for my little grand-daughter. What will you take for the place?' "

184

Mrs. Apodaca gasped and tied another knot in the corner of her shawl. Carmencita sat bolt upright, her eyes as big as winter stars. "What did you say, Señora?" she shrilled.

I said, "This is my home. It is not for sale."

"What did the Texan say to that?" she piped.

"He said, 'Come, come, everything has its price.' "

"What did you say then?" begged Carmencita and Cousin Canuto in one breath.

"I laughed and said, 'All right! One hundred thousand dollars!' The man from Texas looked a bit hysterical as he glanced at the little adobe house and me. Then he backed his Cadillac down the driveway at such speed that he almost took off a corner of the violinist's house. But they waved friendly hands as they left and I could hear them laughing together."

"At that it wasn't too high a price," ejaculated Cousin Canuto, "if you know what Carmencita knows, Señora."

"Let me tell, let me tell," shrilled Carmencita.

"It was almost dark one night just before the big snow and I was going up the footpath along the little ditch. In the dirt road that ends in front of your place, were three men walking up and down. Two were carrying heavy shovels. The other one had strapped around his waist what must have been a new kind of geiger counter. It even had earphones so he could hear the clicks better. He put an extension from the counter on the dirt road, listened hard, and said, 'Dig here.' Then they walked a few steps more, and he listened and said, 'Dig here.' It went on and on like that. At last I heard them say, 'This is it.' "

"Now you can sell your place for ten times one hundred thousand dollars," interrupted Cousin Canuto. "So can the Apodacas and the Seguras and maybe even I who live only a mile beyond."

We sat in a brittle silence. It is not pleasant to prick a balloon full of dreams. "Those men were not uranium scouts," I explained as gently as possible. "They are city employees. That contraption was not a geiger counter. It was a machine to locate a metal manhole cover that gets buried with adobe mud on our dirt roads. And besides, I hope not one ounce of uranium will be found within a hundred miles of our old town. It would spoil everything. So far as I have heard, we do not need to worry."

Mrs. Apodaca calmly picked out the knots she had tied in the corner of her shawl. With a note of relief in her voice she murmured, *"Bueno,* now none of us weel have to move away!"

Cousin Canuto steadied himself in a moment and repeated *"Bueno,* I see now how much we might lose, Señora." But Carmencita looked somewhat deflated for weeks as she passed my exclamatory windows.

GARDENER ON HORSEBACK
INCORPORATED

*E*arly in a shell-tinted morning last spring, before I was fully awake, someone on horseback cantered smartly down my driveway. Morning after morning this happened. Years ago, when I first moved into the Little Adobe House, people on horseback passed up and down my driveway. So did burros and occasional goats. But of late years my long driveway has turned into a much-used footpath for people, cats, dogs and *muchachos* bent on their small affairs.

All through the passing days, I watched for the early-morning equestrian to make the return trip and clear up the mystery. But he did not return. I have learned to accept the small mysteries of Tenorio Flat with increasing patience. Eventually they unwind, to my prolonged delight.

The unwinding usually begins with Mrs. Apodaca. With shining eyes and with pride written all over her small brown face, she exclaimed from the comfortable depths of the big rocker, "Ah, Señora, my Cousin Canuto ees the smart man. He have start a fine new business and make much *dinero.*"

She untied a corner of her black shawl and produced a cheap little card, poorly printed with the cryptic words, "Gardener On Horseback Incorporated." That was all.

"Do you mean," I gasped, "that Cousin Canuto rakes, hoes, and cuts lawns from the saddle?"

"But no, Señora," giggled Mrs. Apodaca. "Horseback ees the way he come and go to and from hees work. Already he breeng electric wire to hees *casita.* He buy María Lupita fine new beeg wash-machine—ten dollars down and ten a month unteel paid."

"Where, in that little house crammed with nine people, could she put a washing machine?" I demanded.

"Een the leetle store," nodded Mrs. Apodaca. "She seet in chair that rock while machine work and she take care of leetle store at same time. Wheen she ees not using wash-machine, other señoras een *placita* bring bundles and use wash-machine and pay leetle money to María Lupita. Already she buy black lace scarf to wear on head in summer instead of black shawl. Sundays only!"

At this, Mrs. Apodaca started for home. "But why," I stayed her flight, "does not Cousin Canuto return at night through my yard?"

"Because," exulted Mrs. Apodaca, "he go home by way of beeg market to buy meat and other nize things to eat."

Evidently she told her famous cousin that I would appreciate a visit on horseback, as he stopped by after buying groceries.

He was wearing his customary faded blue jeans and work shirt open at the throat with a red bandanna knotted for a neckerchief and another dangling from a trouser pocket. On his head was a torn-brimmed old straw hat with little yellow roses tucked under the faded and frayed ribbon around the crown. From a dilapidated wallet he handed me one of the cards which proclaimed his new enterprise, "Gardener On Horseback Incorporated."

"But why on horseback?" I questioned.

"Because where I work, Señora, is long way out, in the hills where piñón and cedar trees grow and rich people coming here build fine new houses and have the big, big yard and the widespread view. I have no *carro,* so I borrow the horse of my *primo,* Pantaleón Padilla, who lives near me."

"But how can he keep a horse in Santa Fe?" I puzzled. "A horse is livestock and livestock is not permitted in the city limits."

"I do not know," smiled Cousin Canuto, unconcerned. "Maybe his *casita* is just over the city line. Maybe Pantaleón never hear of the law. Maybe he know city *político. ¿Quién sabe?*"

Then I noticed that rakes, brooms, hoes, clippers, spray guns and all the paraphernalia of the gardner's trade, were strapped to the back of the saddle and protruded widely on either side of his mount. "Don't those rich people have their own shovels and things?"

"Of course, of course," soothed Cousin Canuto. "They have every device to save the labor—the lawnmower that go by motor, the automatic water system, the spray that go by motor, everything that money can buy. All those old tools and my *guitarra* are *la atmósfera* which those new people want so much.

"I give them the old-time touch. Even their little children follow me around while I work. When I finish my lunch and take siesta in shady

spot, *naturalmente* I strum a little on my *guitarra*.
Out come all the people and sit around on grass
and listen. So now when they have company for
lunch, they give me ten dollars extra to play my
guitarra under the window. And the company
say, 'What an atmosphere has old Santa Fe!'

"Soon as I get electric wire and wash-
machine paid for, I build big adobe room for my
older boys, the ones in the newspaper business.
My third boy has now entered the profession and
I am helping him buy his delivery bicycle—ten
dollars down and ten a month. After that is paid
for," continued Cousin Canuto, "I shall buy—"

"But summer is short in this high altitude.
Soon you can do no garden work."

"No, no, Señora," broke in Cousin Canuto.
"In the autumn come the rake the leaves and
plant the bulbs. When snow come I sweep the
walks and shovel the driveways and bring in
wood for fireplaces, big ones, not corner. And at
Christmas ten thousand *farolitos,* made of lighted
candle in sand in paper bag, will go up on those
fine roof tops. And little piñón fires burning red
in the night will line those fine cément driveways.
And I and my *guitarra* will be in great demand
to sing the old Spanish Christmas songs at many
a fine party."

192

Cousin Canuto leaned toward me and whispered, "That *atmósfera* which is all around us in Santa Fe is a rich gold mine—not as rich as uranium, but much more pleasant."

At that, the Gardener On Horseback cantered briskly up my driveway, hoes, rakes and shovels rattling merrily as he rode.

LA ATMÓSFERA
AND PETUNIAS

*W*hen Mrs. Apodaca comes dragging her feet down my driveway, when she totters into the Little Adobe House there to sink limply into the old rocker, I am not too concerned. Through the years I have learned that my neighbor takes all big misfortunes on an even keel. Small misfortunes are just an opportunity for her to indulge her superb sense of the dramatic.

"Those two Abeyta boys have come back to Santa Fe at the same time," she sobbed. "That beeg one, Abundio, have three-week vacation from airport in Arizona where he work hees way to be Space pilot. He have plenty *dinero* een fine new wallet. And just when I theenk I have Carmencita down out of Space to learn to paint the pretty picture weeth Mees Lucretia Wintermoot!

And Young Mr. Abeyta ees home for all summer from the School of the Farming where he have free lessons, but no *dinero*—not one dime. He look for work but cannot find. Already that Abundio take Carmencita to three movies, one dance and seven sodas of the ice cream."

Mrs. Apodaca wiped her eyes with the flour sack that bound her head like a nun's wimple. "The papá of those boys leeve on *ranchito* a few miles out of Santa Fe. The papá let Abundio have old *Fordcito* to come to town. Young Mr. Abeyta having no *dinero* for *gasolina,* ride een on old horse hees papá let heem use. Those boys! First one pop-pops up to my *casita* een old *Fordcito,* and then the other clumps-clumps up on old horse. Each one say same theeng, 'Where ees Carmencita?'

"I say Carmencita paint the pretty picture weeth Mees Lucretia Wintermoot—maybe along *Acequia,* maybe on Pecos Road, maybe I know not where. *Ay de mí,* Señora, no matter how early Young Mr. Abeyta start out on horseback, Abundio hear heem and get *Fordcito* and pass heem on highway weeth toots of deesdain."

Mrs. Apodaca tottered homeward to reappear with smiling face and twinkling eyes a few days later. "I say to Mees Lucretia Wintermoot, 'Why not find new place to paint? Eees nize place een hills back of Tesuque. But you weel have to climb steep trail on foot.' So she hire Ambrosio to drive them out and carry easels and lonch I pack for them up steep trail.

"Wheen Abundio rattle up een *Fordcito* and ask where ees Carmencita, I say, 'On peekneek weeth Mees Lucretia Wintermoot where they walk long way up steep trail.' I guessed right, Señora! Peoples weeth thoughts soaring een Space do not like to use feet to climb dirt trail. Abundio shake head and say ees too hot day to walk. But wheen Young Mr. Abeyta ask and I say where, he smile and start out as fast as old horse can go. I call after heem, 'I pack lonch for you, too.'

"Mees Lucretia tale me what happen on peekneek. More happen than I theenk. Young Mr. Abeyta ride horse to foot of trail and walk up where she and Carmencita paint the pretty picture. He look at picture and weenk at Mees Lucretia and say, 'Look nize on wall of leetle adobe house on *rancho* some day. Oh, eef I could find job here thees summer and not have to go far, far away!'

"So Mees Lucretia say that Cousin Canuto, the Gardener On Horseback, ees looking for

196

someone to help heem take care of reech people's yards. He have more work than he can do. But hees helper must have horse and also *la atmósfera*.

"Young Mr. Abeyta say, 'I have horse all right, but what ees thees *atmósfera* theeng?'

"Carmencita grin and say, 'You have to look quaint and play the *guitarra* while you hoe the weed.'

"Young Mr. Abcyta say sadly, 'I can wcar my old *vaquero* hat and my silver concha belt, but play the *guitarra* I cannot nor seeng any more than a creeket.' Then he brighten up and say, 'But I know more how to make lawns and flowers grow than anyone in Santa Fe. Let Cousin Canuto geeve them *la atmósfera*. I weel geeve them petunias.'

"He deed not wait to eet the lonch I pack for heem. He was down the trail and galloping away to find Cousin Canuto. Een no time he was back, grinning from ear to ear. Cousin Canuto hired heem."

Mrs. Apodaca sat rocking triumphantly in the old rocker so recently the scene of one of her dramas of despair. "Young Mr. Abeyta went to work the next day. Not only weel he keep that Carmencita from going up een Space, but he weel have *dinero* for the movie, for the dance and for

197

the soda of the ice cream. And more than that, Señora, he save Cousin Canuto's fine business."

"I thought everything was going fine for Gardener On Horseback Incorporated," I gasped.

"That very day," whispered Mrs. Apodaca, "Pantaleón Padilla say to Cousin Canuto that someone in City Hall find out that hees house ees een city leemits where cannot keep horse. So Pantaleón Padilla say to Cousin Canuto that he weel have to take horse he let heem have out to *ranchito* of *compadre* who leeve far, far away.

"Poor Cousin Canuto theenk and theenk what to do. Ees too far to walk to work. No bus goes near. Bicycle like boy een newspaper business ees no good. Nor ees old *carro,* ten dollars down and ten a month teel paid. No one of these ways have *la atmósfera.* Hees customers weel not hire heem weethout *atmósfera.* Hees fine business ees ruin!

"So he find Young Mr. Abeyta and say that their fine business ees ruin and why. And Young Mr. Abeyta theenk one *momento* and then laugh and say, 'That ees easy, Cousin Canuto. I'll ride home weeth you at night and lead the horse of Pantaleón Padilla to the *ranchito* of my papá weech ees not een the leemits of Santa Fe. Een

198

the morning I weel lead the horse to your *casita*. We weel ride side by side down the highway weeth two sets of hoes, shovels, rakes, and cleepers going cleekety-clack. Everyone weel stop and stare. Eet weel be the good advertise. What a sight eet weel be for those peoples een fine new houses wheen they see two gardeners tie two horses to their juniper trees. *Atmósfera!* And beeg, beeg petunias!' "

THE BROOM
BEHIND THE DOOR

$\mathcal{T}$hese summer afternoons, I often find myself sitting in Mrs. Apodaca's small kitchen. It is a pleasant place to sit with yellow Castile roses tossing their fragrance through the deep-set windows. Even with the door closed, from the adjoining room comes the indistinguishable ebb and flow of adolescent chatter, the ripple of giggles followed by soaring laughter.

"That Carmencita" has reached the gregarious years. In between babysitting, contesting, selling small articles from door-to-door and stepping out with Young Mr. Abeyta, Carmencita runs with the pack. Usually their meeting place is her mother's small front room. Some days Carmencita wears old faded blue jeans, shapeless sweaters, and sloppy scuffers. Others days she reverts to the military and strides about, correctly turned out in near-military attire. Sometimes she goes to a dance, swirling pink silk and net with silver slippers winging her steps. All her days have become so entrancing that she wants to play every part on the stage—in appropriate costume.

Mrs. Apodaca takes it all in stride with the calm confidence of a woman who knows she is mistress of the situation. After all, she has experienced a milder version of all this before with Lupe, Luz, and Armendita. Usually about four o'clock the crowd leaves en masse with a final crescendo of giggles and a firm resolve to see some "perfectly-out-of-this-world" movie come Saturday.

"That pack certainly knows enough to leave at a reasonable hour," I commented. "Did you tell them or did you lay down the law to Carmencita?"

Mrs. Apodaca's eyes twinkled and she hid a smile behind her hand. "I do not tale Carmencita. But they go. I just put a broom behind the door."

"You mean if they didn't go, you would sweep them out?" I cried aghast.

"They do not know there ees a broom behind the door. Neither does Carmencita! But eet works. Eet has always worked. Only we Spanish people from the leetle villages know about the broom behind the door. Always, Señora, if you want peoples to leave and not seet and seet, day or night, put a broom behind the door."

"What kind of a broom and what door?" I demanded thinking of a few people who were inclined to "seet and seet" until long past midnight.

"Oh, any old broom and any door in the house where eet can't be seen, Señora. Of course," she added, "eef you want someone to stay long time, remember to take broom from behind door."

Mrs. Apodaca's big eyes twinkled more and more, her small hands fluttered as she talked and laughed at the same time. "When that nize boy, Young Mr. Abeyta, come to see Carmencita, I always remember to take the broom from behind the door so he can stay as long as he like. He has good job weeth Cousin Canuto thees summer, but he work so hard he do not get over to see us very often.

"But when that older brother of hees, that *muy guapo*—handsome—Abundio, come to see Carmencita to talk about Space, I always put the broom back behind the door. That Spaceman! Abundio, he come and come at least once a week while he is on vacation from airport in Arizona. But always, Señora, he go at nine o'clock. He do

202

not want to go, but he go, he know not why. Eet ees that broom behind the door."

"Behind what door did you put it?" I asked.

"I put my broom, an old worn-out broom in the corner of my *ropería*, clothes closet, een my bedroom where no one can see. Eet work just as good as anywhere," exulted Mrs. Apodaca.

Musing over the ability of an old broom in a *ropería*, I remarked that she was very long-suffering to give up her own front room so many afternoons and evenings to Carmencita's callers.

"I like better here anyway," she confided. "But one theeng I put the feet on. I weel not let Carmencita make Gracie-us Leeving een my front room. She want to make Hollywood drapes out of flimsy stuff instead of fiesta print. She want to take out good bed I paint green and make into couch weeth hand-woven blanket and pay hundred dollars for something all covered weeth what she call foam of the rubber. I weel not take down beeg picture of me and *el papá* at time of our wedding. I weel not take down pictures of *mi mamá y mi papá*. Fine beeg pictures! I weel not change one theeng, Señora."

Just then Carmencita in near-military uniform came striding into the room. Evidently she was expecting Abundio, the Spaceman, that evening. Her mother advised a handful of cookies, *bizcochitos,* and then said, winking slyly at me, "Carmencita, please go to my *ropería* and get the old worn-out broom you find there. I want to show it to the Señora who has much pleasure een old theengs."

Carmencita looked somewhat confused. "Oh, that old broom! I was looking for something in your *ropería,* Mamacita, and I took it out, oh, over a month ago. I didn't think it was any good and gave it to little Eloy Alarid for a broomstick horse. His papá carved a little wooden head and screwed it on one end of the broomstick and made a rope tail for the other. Eloy calls his horse Caddy, short for Cadillac."

After Carmencita left, Mrs. Apodaca sat quietly as the full implications of Carmencita's removal of the old broom dawned on both of us. But Mrs. Apodaca's folklore was not to be so easily toppled. "Anyway," she said, "you try eet, Señora. Eet always work, that broom behind the door."

STRATEGY WITH EARRINGS

"Ah," exclaimed Mrs. Apodaca, sinking into the big rocker, "how good a summer! Everytheeng grow beeg weeth much rain—flowers and weeds like a wilderness. Young Mr. Abeyta and Cousin Canuto make much *dinero* as Gardener on Horseback Incorporated. Young Mr. Abeyta go back to the school of the farming weeth many dollars even eef he and Carmencita go to dances, go to movies and have the soda of the ice cream many, many times. Before he go, Señora, he geeve Carmencita very nize present, the jewelry of the costume—a beeg peen weeth blue and diamondlike stones that sparkle, a reeng for the feenger and reengs for the ears. I tell Carmencita she can wear all that jewelry of the costume but the reengs for the ears. I do not like the reengs for the ears."

Mrs. Apodaca shook an adamant head and at that her own earrings of soft old gold swayed in shimmering arcs.

"All the young girls and their mothers, too, wear the costume jewelry now," I protested. "It is very pretty. It accents the color of the dress and highlights the face. Why can't Carmencita wear the earrings along with the pin and the finger ring and the bracelet?"

"Because," said Mrs. Apodaca, folding her lips decisively, "I do not like the way they are fastened to the ear. They are *de ruda magnificencia*, they are barbaric."

"But how do you fasten your own earrings?" I demanded, watching the swaying golden circlets.

"I have my ears pierced wheen I am a girl," Mrs. Apodaca proclaimed. "My own earrings are not held on weeth screws. Those screws in ears make ladies do strange theengs, Señora. I see you do not wear earrings ever. So you do not know. But the next time you are out weeth Anglo ladies weeth earrings, just watch for a funny look that comes on the face. The screw on the ear ees uncomfortable and the lady wonders what causes eet. She gazes into space weeth expression blank. She sees not, she hears not. Then suddenly she know what ees bothering her. She unscrew ear-ring or she tighten eet so weel stay on ear. Some-times weethout knowing what she do, she take off earring and put eet down on top of bookcase or on table or on shelf of adobe fireplace."

Mrs. Apodaca sighed, "Wheen I go to help Mees Boggers get house een order after party, *teléfono* reeng and reeng. 'Mees Boggers,' a voice weel say, 'deed you or your maid find a yellow-and-purple earring anywhere? No, no, I cannot remember where I left eet. Maybe was on your dressing table, maybe on tea-table, maybe on that darlings square piano.'

"We look and look. Sometimes we find. Sometimes we do not. Then wheen Mees Boggers say we cannot find, sometimes a voice weel say, 'Are you sure that maid of yours ees honest?' Mees Boggers get so angry and so excite, she collapse and I have to do all the work.

"But," continued Mrs. Apodaca, "*teléfono* reengs off and on all day. When I say that Mees Boggers ees collapse, they tale me where to look for earrings. I find one een woodbasket by fire-place where eet has fallen from table and another under pillow on sofa. No, Señora, I weel not let Carmencita get shedding habits weeth earrings like those Anglo ladies."

At this, Mrs. Apodaca wrapped her shawl about her so tightly it looked like a kind of armor. Thus supported, she stalked homeward, a fortress of a woman.

Carmencita dropped by the next day to show me the pin on her dress, the ring on her finger and the bracelet on her wrist. Then she reached into her purse and took out a tissue-wrapped box which contained the forbidden earrings. Big as half dollars they were, and heavy with blue and diamondlike stones. Tears filled her eyes as she explained that, beautiful as they were, she could not wear them. *Mamacita* would never relent. She would have to write to Young Mr. Abeyta and explain why she could never wear the fine earrings.

A couple of weeks later, Mrs. Apodaca and Carmencita came together to see me. In Carmencita's small brown ears twinkled the great blue and diamondlike earrings. All the sunlight in the room seemed centered in them and in her happy eyes.

Dazzled by them, it was some time before I noticed that Mrs. Apodaca was not wearing the customary big circlets of soft old gold in her ears. In the shadow of her black shawl discreetly shone silver and turquoise earrings to match the great ring she wears for all state occasions.

208

At my surprised glance, Mrs. Apodaca laughed with delight. "Such fine earrings," she exclaimed, turning her head from side to side so that I might get the full effect. "Young Mr. Abeyta sent them to me weeth a letter. He bought them from a Nabahoo man who ees famous for making fine jewelry. Young Mr. Abeyta say in hees letter they are to say thank you for helping heem to get a good job weeth Cousin Canuto."

Where, I wondered, had Young Mr. Abeyta found earrings in this day and age that were made for pierced ears? Perhaps they had been made to order.

Carmencita twinkled with laughter at my puzzled face. As they were leaving, she hesitated before the tin-framed mirror to look at her own jewel-decorated ears. "I like them big, big," she exclaimed. "And even mamacita says they are pretty, but not as pretty as hers."

As her mother disappeared around the corner of the Little Adobe House, Carmencita flung her arms about me and whispered, "Mamacita's earrings are held on by screw fastenings just like mine. And never a peep out of her!"

*O*ne May evening, when the lilac hedge was in full purple bloom against a taller background of pink-tinted apple blossoms, Mrs. Apodaca blew like a small black cloud into the Little Adobe House. She dropped limply into the big rocker and wept with a fine sense of the dramatic into one of Mr. Apodaca's red bandannas with which she had thoughtfully provided herself.

"*Ay,* Señora," she sobbed, "that Mees Boggers ees going to move away from Santa Fe—far, far away. She try to keep Santa Fe quaint. She try her best. She weel not buy one theeng in stores along the Plaza that have light of the neon. She get many peoples to join 'Bird Watchers, Unite.' But weeth parking meters, weeth traffic lights, weeth peoples building strange houses in every direction, Mees Boggers can no longer take eet."

I knew there were no words that could miti-
gate Mrs. Apodaca's woe. Years ago when Miss
Boggers retired from an Eastern industrial city
and fled to Santa Fe to fill in the gaps and crevices
of her hard-working years with the charm of our
old town and some versification of her own, Mrs.
Apodaca, oddly enough, found charm and poetry
in Miss Boggers herself. Miss Bogger's raveling
museumlike adobe, her social and artistic adven-
tures, represented romance to Mrs. Apodaca. No
one could take her place.

"Mees Boggers find nize old-time adobe
casita een leetle town near Taos," continued Mrs.
Apodaca. "She put up much money to hold that
casita unteel she can sell her place in Santa Fe.
Many peoples like that *casita*. Every time someone like that place and say weel buy, Mees Boggers raises price five hundred dollars. But steel
peoples want eet. They say, 'How darlings, how
sweet!' "

What was my surprise within a few days, to
welcome a radiant Mrs. Apodaca who almost
skimmed across my threshold. Rolling sparkling
eyes, fluttering small brown hands, Mrs. Apodaca
fairly sang, "Mees Boggers ees not going to move
away from Santa Fe. She do not care eef she lose
money she pay down on *casita* een leetle town

211

near Taos. She weel stay here always. Sometheeng happen that could only happen een Santa Fe. Sometheeng happen that change her mind."

"What happened?" I puzzled.

"Was *música,*" explained Mrs. Apodaca, humming a gay little tune of her own.

"Music! There's always music in Santa Fe. How could that make her change her plans and take a heavy loss in money on the option she took on the house near Taos?"

"That *música* come two times close together. *Música* follow *música.*"

"What kind of music was it? Even around here, almost every day or night one can hear guitar music or the violinist practicing or radio music seeping out of every house in Tenorio Flat."

Mrs. Apodaca giggled and settled herself for an unhurried dissertation. "You know that boy, Trinidád, of Cousin Canuto who ees een newspaper business? He deleever paper to Mees Boggers. Eees rainy day and he prop up bicycle and hand paper to Mees Boggers so eet weel not get wet and muddy. Ees good newspaper man, that Trinidád."

Resignedly I leaned back in my chair. This would probably continue half the night.

Mrs. Apodaca smiled benignly. "Wheen Trinidád hand paper to Mees Boggers, she theenk she hear *música* but she cannot tale from where eet come. Wheen Trinidád peek up bicycle she know. That *música* come from bicycle of Trinidád. So Trinidád show her how he have carry-around *rahdio* een bag where he carry papers. He say he have to pedal that bicycle many miles over bad roads and carry beeg load of papers. So he buy carry-around *rahdio* for thirty-seven dollars and feefty cents. On time! Now he do not mind chuckholes een road nor mud nor dust nor heavy load of papers nor ladies cross wheen paper ees late nor beeg dog that try to bite hees leg. He have *música* weeth heem."

"A worthy son of Cousin Canuto," I rejoiced.

Mrs. Apodaca nodded happily and relaxed in her chair. Minutes ticked by in profound silence. "Didn't you say there was some more music?" I suggested.

Mrs. Apodaca rallied slightly. "Do you remember Hipólito, Señora? He used to peek up the waste in our trash cans and always ran away weeth the leeds because he was *preocupado* weeth the songs he makes to seeng at the wedding and for fiestas in leetle towns?"

"Of course I remember Hipólito."

I smiled at the recollection of Hipólito who had absentmindedly loaded the lid of "Mees" Boggers' new waste can onto his truck. After "Mees" Boggers had spent weeks calling the Department of Sanitation, Hipólito returned that lid to her with a triumphant flourish—in the hotel lobby where she was meeting very special friends from her home town of Detroit. "Mees" Boggers had been very chagrined.

"I've often wondered what became of Hipólito."

Mrs. Apodaca laughed. "Hipólito steel works peeking up garbage trash for Santa Fe but not for us. But he peeks up Mees Boggers' trash. A beeg new truckie now drives right up to her gate and when Hipólito dumps the waste into the white truckie, the driver watch to see that Hipólito put leed back on Mees Boggers' waste can.

"Mees Boggers was standing by her gate wheen beeg waste truckie came. Hipólito jump out and emptied her waste can and climb back on truckie. Eet was then that Mees Boggers theenk she hear *música*. First she theenk eet ees Trinidád coming back on hees bicycle. Then she theenk ees from house next door. But eet ees not. She go

214

up to truckie and look een and see carry-around *rahdio* wheech ees playing softly.

" 'Eet ees Hipólito's *rahdio,*' say truckie driver. 'He buy eet for thirty-five dollars and feefty cents. On time! Then Hipólito drive off een truckie to the *música* of *Cielito Lindo.* They wave happily to Mees Boggers as they pass.

"Wheen Mees Boggers tale me about *música,* she ees geeving her rhubarb plants a good watering. 'Here I stay, Mrs. Apodaca,' she say. 'Where else in the world can one get hees daily paper to the sound of *música* and even hees garbage picked up to the soft *música* of *Cielito Lindo?*' "

WARP AND WEFT

$\mathcal{J}$ust before Christmas one year, Tenorio Flat rocked with the breath-taking news that Sergeant Segura had given his papá and mamacita a television set. It was the first one to appear in their midst. Women left their *bizcochito*-making, men left their woodchopping, and *los muchachos* left their wintry games to stand awe-struck in the elder Seguras' crooked little adobe, there to marvel at this new evidence of Sergeant Segura's nobility.

There in the little crooked room, amid the poorest of furnishings, stood the masterpiece with not an atom of dust on its shining surface. Speechless with pride and delight, Señor and Señora Segura tiptoed around the marvel, pointing with shaking fingers to the size of the screen and the luster of the finish.

Suddenly I realized that I had seen no shining antenna atop the sagging roof of the little

216

crooked house. "You will have to wire your house for electricity," I exclaimed.

Señor and Señora Segura shook determined heads. "But no, Señora! We would not like the big bills from the electric company. We will look at this so-fine Christmas present from our son and then he can take it to his *casita,* which have the electric wire. When he have time, once in a while, he will drive us over to his *casita* in the *automóvil* he gave us for *aniversario* present, and we can enjoy it with him and Little Teresa of Tucumcari and those twin *angelitas* of theirs."

I was face-to-face with the fact that Sergeant Segura had not only given his parents an *automóvil* which neither of them could operate for an *aniversario* present, but also a television set for "Creesmas" for which they had no electricity.

These facts had evidently permeated the thought of several wage-earning "sohns" of Tenorio Flat whose parents received no such gifts from them. "It's easy enough to give your papá and mamacita presents which they can never use, but which you can," they pointed out. "And they call that smart fellow noble!"

I must confess that during the past few months I had noticed that the *aniversario automóvil* had frequently been absent from the evergreen-thatched *ramada* Señor Segura had built over it. With twin babies, the younger Seguras doubtless put that *automóvil* to good use. But with these few exceptions, Tenorio Flat remained loyal to that estimable young man, Sergeant Segura.

Often in this region, the course of events seems as devoid of pattern as the newly strung loom of a native weaver when he starts to ply his winging shuttle. Usually, if one has patience, color begins to blend with color and line meets line and design appears. But the design of the Segura family remained a mystery.

By early spring my attention had wandered to another intriguing subject. One day I noticed a couple of native workmen atop the leaking roof of an ancient adobe house on the edge of Tenorio Flat. It was an unusually attractive old building, long and low built in the shape of a letter L. No one had lived in it since I could remember. Most of the adobe bricks along the roofline had disintegrated. The outside adobe plaster was about all gone. There were few unbroken windows in the whole house. But even among the wreckage of the years it showed good lines, and it boasted fine sturdy projecting *vigas,* and two charming corner fireplaces.

The workmen evidently knew adobe construction after the old manner. Weather-frayed bricks came out of the walls and were replaced by good new hand-made ones. A new roof replaced the sagging, storm-rotted tarpaper. The whole outside received a new rosy coat of smooth adobe plaster. Inside walls were repaired and glistened with fresh white calsomine. New glass went into many-paned window casements, painted blue within and without.

Electric wiring was brought in from a pole down the street. Ditches were dug to connect with gas and water lines. Evidently the new owner had modern ideas as well as loyalty for old beauties. There followed bathroom equipment, an electric refrigerator and washing machine, a tiny gas range for summer cooking and an enormous old-fashioned iron cookstove for winter. "An artist is moving in," I thought, "one who knows this region."

Then one day as I was passing, up drove a plumber's truck and out jumped Sergeant Segura. "Señora," he shouted, "did you know I am now a licensed plumber? I go to night school all last year. I now make three-fifty an hour and someday I'll have my own little shop." Brandishing a kit of tools, he headed into the old adobe.

"Who had the good sense to buy and restore this old adobe?" I asked.

"I did," grinned the noble Sergeant. "Teresa and I did not fit well into that house in the sub-division. So we sold it and move in here next week. The big yard will be fine for the babies and *mi papá* and *mamacita* live right back there down the alley. When I get a sapling fence built all around the yard, I'll make a little blue gate so we can go back and forth easy."

Sergeant Segura's contemporaries no longer laugh and slap one another on the back about his gifts to his parents. The *aniversario automóvil* rolls out loaded with senior and junior Seguras. Often of an autumn afternoon I see Señor and Señora Segura sitting before the corner fireplace in their son's new, old *casita*. Each has an *angelita* on a knee, while the "Creesmas" TV produces its drama of song, story, and "curren' events." The Segura pattern is complete.

The Segura pattern is but an example of what has been happening in this region for countless ages, from pit-house Indians to the coming of the Spanish and to the roll of wagon wheels down the Santa Fe Trail. Always the warp of design, anchored to lofty mountains, limitless sky, and enormous space, has held true and strong. Only the weft has changed to blend new colors and evolve new lines of another newer design.

*I*n addition to the pattern of its three peoples—Indian, Spanish, and northern European—New Mexico shows other threads of design running through the weft and warp of its cultural weaving. They are like the "spirit line" Indians weave into their blankets and baskets or the "heart line" the women of Zia paint on their bird-decorated pottery.

It is one thing to know with the intellect that our Indian population probably came over from Asia by way of the Bering Strait dim ages ago. It is another to pick up that golden Oriental thread oneself, thousands of years later; or to discern the Moorish thread which came in with Spanish colonists four centuries ago. Originating half a world apart, Asian and Moorish threads unite in design here to give meaning and portent to the underlying pattern. They came in when distance was a prodigious barrier, when men walked a continent's length or waited for winds to fill galleon sails. They were carried in the heart.

I picked up my first Oriental thread when I saw the Indians atop lofty Ácoma Rock give the Butterfly Dance on my first Christmas in New Mexico. The men dancers stamping out the measures to roaring rawhide drums were Indians—First Americans. But the women dancers presented the Asian thread. With cerise circles painted on either cheek, with black, purple-highlighted hair flowing over brilliant back-shawls of silk and satin, in hand-woven kirtles and knee-high white boots, they did all their dancing with outstretched arms and hands holding bunches of blue spruce. "This is not America," I kept saying. "This is Asia."

Other threads I found as years went by and always with a sense of exultation. One day, in the Museum of Navajo Ceremonial Arts, I discovered some exquisite silver and turquoise jewelry. By this time I knew that the turquoise is the sacred stone of the Indians and that quantities of beads, some mosaics and pendants of the skystone had been discovered in prehistoric ruins, but that turquoise combined with silver, as we know it today, is a fairly recent craft dating from Spanish settlement days.

"Who made that gorgeous turquoise and silver jewelry?" I asked the curator, "Navajos or Zuñis?"

"Neither," he laughed. "Some of it came from Tibet and some from Mongolia."

We talked with delight about the Oriental thread continually appearing in our strange, lovely land. "Some Japanese students were here a few years ago," he added. "We took them to Zuñi where they speak a language that seems to have little connection with the other Indian languages of the region. When we got Zuñis and Japanese together we were amazed to see how much they resembled one another. But most amazing was that the Zuñis understood some Japanese words and the Japanese some Zuñi words."

And then I remember the little Chinese woman who visited Santa Fe after the war. She was an exchange student whose destination was an Eastern university. But she had read a little about the New Mexican Indians and had turned aside on her own planning. "How can I see some Indians?" was her one request. We took her to Picurís Pueblo, high in the wooded mountains near Taos, to see the Feast Day Dance.

The Indians of Picurís formed admiring circles about the little Chinese woman. She was

224

dressed in modified Chinese costume of black brocade with long flowing sleeves and upstanding collar. Once in awhile she asked a question. After profound deliberation, an older Indian would answer. Then they would all smile at one another. It was as if they had a secret understanding and were remembering half-forgotten things. As we drove home through the gilded wastelands, happy tears rolled down her cheeks. "Today, today," she whispered, "I have been home in China."

She disappeared after that and people in Santa Fe were quite concerned. They did not believe that she had proceeded to her Eastern university without saying farewell. At last, after some searching, she was found in a lower Rio Grande Indian pueblo. She was sitting at the large kitchen table of one of the old adobe houses. Newspapers had been pasted together and she was busily cutting out the pattern of her Chinese costume which the Indian women of the pueblo admired and wished to duplicate.

The Moorish thread in the region came in with early Spanish colonists whose homeland had long known the imprint of North Africa. Thence came a knowledge of thick-walled earthen homes, of irrigation by an intricate system of meandering water ditches, of wall-protected, flower-fragrant patios. Oddly enough, they found many of these North African importations already in use in modified form in a Red Man's world.

One bleak November day, I stood shivering along the edge of the dance plaza in Jemez Pueblo. Snow was falling on the high peaks back of us and on the red, red cliffs. Suddenly came the sound of music—not the customary spine-tickling roar of Indian drums, but the stringed notes of Spanish violin and guitar. As if blown by the wintry wind, Indians floated down the gusty plaza. On their heads were Moorish headdresses. Their white costumes floating in the wind gave the effect of something ethereal as if the bronze-faced dancers felt no pull of gravity. The Matachines Dance, given by American Indians in a land where dim old trails meet, derives from North Africa through ancient Spain.

What roots men had when they walked a continent's length or waited for breezes to fill a clumsy galleon's sails! What deep roots had the woman who tucked a battered, leather-bound Lindley Murray reader in her capacious pocket before she took her seat in a covered wagon!

The luggage men carry in their hearts is light, but it remains luminous for ages and centuries.

226

HAVING THE YEARS

*L*ike miniature suns, golden roses of Castile framed a wide-open window of the Little Adobe House. At an opposite window, the locust tree was dabbling white fingers of bloom in green pools of foliage. All was as quiet as the depths of some remote mountain glade. It promised to be a good day for catching words.

Suddenly, spoken words in a high treble broke the enfolding quiet. "Hi, Señora, see our hats!"

On tiptoe outside the rose-bounded window stood three small *muchachos* whom I call the three *musketeros*. Each *musketero* had a green paper hat perched rakishly on his head. The hat of Andrés was decorated with yellow dandelions, the hat of Pilar sported one of his sister's hair rib-

bons, but the hat of Agustín bristled with feathers
—russet flicker's feather, blue *piñonero's* feather
and what looked to be tailfeathers from Señor
Segura's black rooster. Agustín departs from the
Murillo cherub type of small *muchacho* preva-
lent in Tenorio Flat. His aunt, Dionisia Delgado,
explains this variation from type by saying with
poorly concealed pride that Agustín had an
Apache Indian chief included with his Spanish
ancestors.

"Run along, *muchachos*," I suggested. "I'm
busy today."

"What are you doing?" demanded Agustín.

"I'm catching words."

"How do you catch words?" persisted the
descendant of the Apache chief.

"With a butterfly net strung with quiet and
beauty."

The three *musketeros* departed reluctantly
for the other side of the house. I had caught perhaps a dozen words when I heard gallopings and
cavortings overhead on the flat roof of the Little
Adobe House. Back and forth charged the three
musketeros, evidently mounted on broomstick
horses. The descendant of the Apache chief
seemed to be leading a spirited attack on a cov-
ered-wagon train crossing the "Sea of Grass." The

228

attackers stamped, they raced back and forth, they uttered bloodcurdling war whoops.

"*Muchachos*," I pleaded, "get down off the roof. Get down and stay down."

Andrés and Pilar, long lashes veiling abashed limpid eyes, let themselves down promptly. But the eyes of Agustín held something of the recent onslaught. "There's a beeg, beeg crack in your roof, Señora. The rain will come in on your *rahdio*, your cat and you. It will, it will!"

Words can seldom be caught by a person who is even slightly irritated. In time, the sight of yellow roses and the musk of locust bloom somewhat allayed the irritation. I had caught a dozen more words when I became aware of an acrid odor mixed with locust musk. Running pellmell toward that odor, I discovered the three *musketeros* around a campfire the fuel for which had been pilfered from my own hoarded stacks. Andrés and Pilar were even then heaping more logs on the blaze, but Agustín sat with one shoe on and one shoe off and the leg and foot without covering protruded stiffly from the shelter of an improvised tent constructed from a Mexican blanket they had taken from my clothesline.

"Look, Señora," urged the faithful retainers, "Chief White Foot sits in the door of his tent."

229

Chief White Foot and his followers were soon ignominiously carrying small buckets of water to put out the soaring flames. Again I returned to the tranquil sight of yellow rose and locust bloom. But I did not catch a single word. Soon I heard the *musketeros* running down the side of my yard which joins the garden of the old rock house. In that garden a little blonde Anglo girl was playing with an elderly cocoa-colored cocker and a very young fox terrier named Mehitabel.

The three *musketeros* stood in a row gazing at the little Anglo girl. She gazed as steadfastly at them. For long minutes they stood taking one another's measure. At last Agustín broke the silence. He spoke in English, but he used the familiar Spanish idiom. "How many years have you?" he asked politely.

"I am six years old," she replied in the English idiom. Then she passed a doll's plate heaped with bright-colored jelly beans. The three *musketeros* accepted but one jelly bean each even in the face of apparent abundance. They were being extremely polite.

Now I needed no butterfly net of quiet and beauty to catch words. The natural childlike question about another child's age had captured more than I could use. The Spanish way of asking a person's age, *"¿Cuántos años tiene él?*—How many years has he?"—in contrast with the English, "How old is he?" seemed the exact difference between having the years and the years having me.

I have had but twenty calendar years in my beloved region, but actually they add up to thousands in new interests, new awareness, and a sense of participation in a vast panorama of people, places, and events. I have held in my hand an Indian artifact, a hide-scraper dropped by some aborigine on a desert trail from seven thousand to ten thousand years ago. With that as a beginning, I have been collecting thousands of years—the white shimmer of cliff dwellings in the rusty-red walls of quicksilver-floored canyons: knee-deep trails worn by Indian feet on blue mesa tops: the Night-Chant of the Navajos in a remote, fire-reddened valley; stone kiva bells of Cuyamunge; weaving hands making visible a dream on the looms of Chimayó; medieval Spanish hymns and pageantry floating across a wintry plaza; old English ballads brought down the Santa Fe Trail in covered wagons; and now the three *musketeros* including Agustín and his Apache chief ancestor.

Because of Pueblo Indian Great-Grand-mother and little Navajo Sam Chee Jo; because of the Apodacas, the Seguras and Cousin Canuto and all they represent, I have the years.